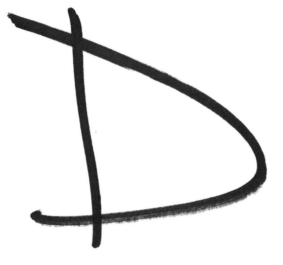

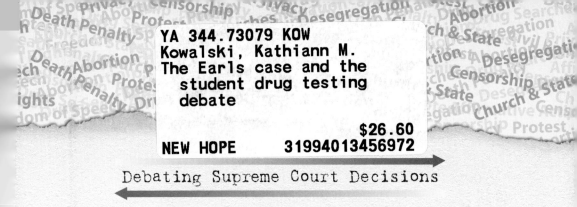

Debating Supreme Court Decisions

The *Earls* Case and the Student Drug Testing Debate

Debating Supreme Court Decisions

Kathiann M. Kowalski

Enslow Publishers, Inc.
40 Industrial Road
Box 398
Berkeley Heights, NJ 07922
USA
http://www.enslow.com

This book is dedicated to my son, Christopher Meissner.

Library of Congress Cataloging-in-Publication Data

Kowalski, Kathiann M., 1955–
    The Earls case and the student drug testing debate : debating Supreme Court decisions
/ Kathiann M. Kowalski.
        p. cm.—(Debating Supreme Court decisions)
    Includes bibliographical references and index.
ISBN 0-7660-2478-4
1. Students—Drug testing—Law and legislation—United States.   2. Students—Civil
rights—United States.   3. Drug testing—Law and legislation—United States.
4. Earls, Lindsay—Trials, litigation, etc.—United States. I. Title. II. Series.
KF4159.K69 2006
344.73'0793—dc22

                        2005034654

Printed in the United States of America

10 9 8 7 6 5 4 3 2 1

To Our Readers: We have done our best to make sure that all Internet Addresses in this book were active and appropriate when we went to press. However, the author and publisher have no control over and assume no liability for the material available on those Internet sites or on other Web sites they may link to. Any comments or suggestions can be sent by e-mail to comments@enslow.com or to the address on the back cover.

Illustration Credits: AP/Wide World, pp. 7, 25, 31, 59, 99; Corbis Images Royalty-Free, p. 19; Hemera Image Express, p. 2; Photos.com, pp. 49, 92; Supreme Court Historical Society, U.S. Supreme Court, Washington, D.C., p. 81; courtesy of Thomas M. Christ, p. 67.

Cover Illustration: Background, Artville; photograph, AP/Wide World.

Contents

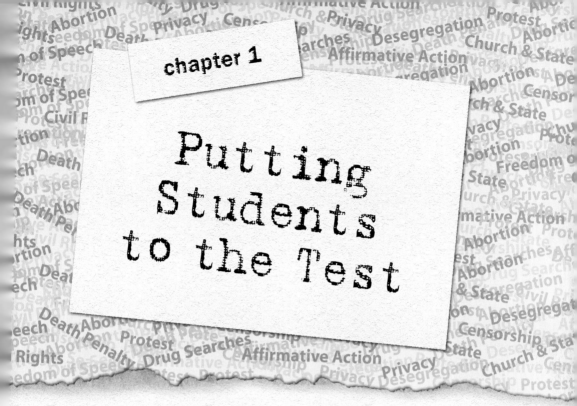

chapter 1

Putting Students to the Test

Lindsay Earls was in music class when a voice over the intercom told the high school sophomore to report to the alumni building. "They might as well have said, 'Lindsay Earls needs to go pee in a cup,'" Lindsay said.[1]

In January 1999, Lindsay Earls was among the students picked for the new random drug testing program at Tecumseh High School in Oklahoma. As she filled a cup with urine, a monitor listened outside the lavatory stall. "It was pretty humiliating," Lindsay said.[2]

Lindsay passed the test. Indeed, no one doubted she would. Lindsay was not a discipline problem. The honor student even described herself as a "goody-two-shoes." "There was no suspicion that I was on drugs whatsoever," Lindsay told reporters.[3]

Lindsay and her parents could have refused the test. But then Lindsay would have had to give up choir, National Honor Society, and her other clubs. "I would have been out of my activities, which is unacceptable to me," she said.[4]

With support from the American Civil Liberties Union (ACLU), Lindsay sued to stop the drug testing program. The case ultimately went to the Supreme Court.

In 2002, the Court ruled against Lindsay and in favor of the school's drug testing program. Since then, more schools have adopted or are looking at programs to test students for drugs. The Court's ruling remains controversial.

To Test or Not to Test

Few people would deny that drug abuse is a serious problem. But drug abuse can be hard to spot.

Herbert Levine was a school superintendent in Salem, Massachusetts. He knows more than most people do about students and drug abuse. Yet it was almost too late before Levine learned his son Joel was addicted to OxyContin, a prescription painkiller. With help, Joel finally got on the road to recovery.

In early 2005, Levine proposed starting a drug testing program in his school district. The program would include all students in sports and other activities. Although the plan might upset some students, Levine felt that the need to protect

Lindsay Earls challenged her school's drug testing program in court, arguing that it infringed on her constitutional rights. She is shown here in 2001.

students justified random drug testing. "Let them be upset, let them moan and complain," he told reporters. "But let them live."[5]

"I've got nothing to hide," senior Erik Groszyk said. "But it seems like they're singling us out because we're high school students and because I'm a high school athlete. Will they do it to teachers as well?"[6]

As of 2004, about 5 percent of America's 15,000 school districts required drug testing for some of their students.[7] Joining that group in 2005 were places like Rigby High School in Idaho,[8] Colleyville Heritage High School in Texas,[9] and Homestead High School in Indiana.[10] The numbers will likely grow. A 2005 New Jersey law set statewide guidelines for schools that want to run drug testing programs.[11]

Meanwhile, other schools stopped student drug testing. In 2003, Janesville, Wisconsin, ended its $20,000 per year testing program. School board member Mike Rundle called it "a waste of time and money."[12]

Politicians are also taking sides. President George W. Bush spoke in favor of student drug testing in his 2004 State of the Union address. That same year, the California state legislature passed a bill that would have banned student drug testing without reasonable suspicion of drug use. However, Governor Arnold Schwarzenegger vetoed the bill. "Specific drug testing policies in schools are locally determined issues," his veto message said. "Therefore, statewide legislation is unnecessary."[13]

Student drug testing programs vary widely. Some schools only test students when they suspect drug or alcohol abuse. In Massachusetts, for example, Framingham High School used Breathalyzer tests at school events only for teens who seemed to have been drinking.[14]

Some schools test students if their parents okay it, but they do not penalize anyone who does not take part. Pennsylvania's Plum School District started such a program in 2004, under which random testing results go only to the parents.[15] Still other schools offer incentives for agreeing to drug testing, such as discounts at area stores.

But a growing number of schools make blanket or random drug testing a condition for taking part in school activities. While some programs use hair or oral fluid samples, urine testing is most common. If students fail a drug test, they face consequences. Schools generally inform parents and require counseling. If later tests are positive, schools may bar students from sports and other activities.

In theory, students and their parents can still refuse such drug testing. However, if they do, students pay a price. They cannot take part in sports or other activities. Such programs are extras and not part of schools' required curricula.

Yet many people feel sports and activities are crucial parts of the school experience. And most competitive colleges look at students' high school activities in the admissions process. Like Lindsay Earls, many students feel they have no choice but to submit to the drug testing.

Important Interests at Stake

Student drug testing programs typically focus on certain illicit drugs—substances that are illegal for people to use and possess. Examples include marijuana, amphetamines, cocaine, opiates, and barbiturates.

Some testing programs also look for signs of alcohol and tobacco use. Most schools forbid students to possess or use these substances on campus. Plus, the law forbids alcohol sales to people under age twenty-one, and stores cannot legally sell tobacco to buyers under eighteen.

On the one hand, school drug testing programs aim to keep students from using illegal and prohibited substances. They also try to identify students who need treatment. Schools want to be drug-free and to protect students.

On the other hand, public schools are government entities. In drug testing programs, the school takes something from a person, such as urine, hair, or oral fluids. Then it has that material analyzed for the presence of specific chemicals.

The results can lead to adverse consequences for students.

Thus, drug testing in public schools is a type of government search and seizure. As such, the Supreme Court has held that it is subject to limits under the Fourth Amendment to the United States Constitution. The Fourth Amendment says:

> The right of the people to be secure in their persons, houses, papers, and effects, against unreasonable searches and seizures, shall not be violated, and no Warrants shall issue, but upon probable cause, supported by Oath or affirmation, and particularly describing the place to be searched, and the persons or things to be seized.

Another important part of the Constitution is the Fourteenth Amendment's Due Process clause. Generally, due process means following rules and procedures designed to ensure fair treatment from the government. Among other things, the Fourteenth Amendment makes the Fourth Amendment's limits binding on states and local governments.

Basically, the Fourth Amendment protects people from unreasonable searches and seizures. In deciding what is reasonable, courts look at the facts and circumstances. They consider judicial precedents—rulings in prior cases that control how the courts should decide future cases. When precedents do not clearly say how courts should rule, judges balance competing interests. They look at the individual interests and expectations of privacy. They consider the government's interest in preventing crime and keeping people safe.

Since 1995, the Supreme Court has twice ruled in favor of student drug testing programs at public schools. *Vernonia School District 47J* v. *Acton* held that a random drug testing program for students in sports programs was constitutional under the Fourth Amendment.[16] In 2002, the Court decided *Board of Education of Independent School District No. 92 of Pottawatomie County* v. *Earls.* The *Earls* case approved a drug testing program for students in all extracurricular activities.[17]

The *Earls* and *Vernonia* cases are presently binding precedent on how the Fourth Amendment applies to student drug testing. That means lower courts must follow them. In both Supreme Court cases, however, the justices split on the issue. In the *Vernonia* case, six justices believed the drug tests were constitutional, while three justices dissented, or disagreed. In the *Earls* case, four justices dissented.

Opinions also vary widely among legal experts, educators, health advocates, and members of the public. The American Civil Liberties Union, the Drug Policy Alliance, and various other groups have publicly criticized student drug testing programs. Organizations supporting drug testing include the Office of National Drug Control Policy and the Student Drug-Testing Coalition.

Student drug testing deals with the schools' relationship to children. Parents trust schools to care for and teach their children. And schools have a strong public interest in keeping children safe. Drug use can endanger both students who use them and other people at the school.

Despite those concerns, children at school have constitutional rights. Courts do not apply those rights as broadly as they do for adults. Among other things, judges know schools need to be run in an orderly way. Thus, schools have broad leeway in maintaining discipline. Yet, students still have rights.

Testing students for drugs creates tension between these broad areas of concern. The conflict is less intense when schools limit testing to cases where they suspect individuals of drug use. Debate becomes more heated when testing policies eliminate the need for individual suspicion. Blanket testing programs collect samples from all students in a group. Random testing involves testing students chosen by chance.

Keep these conflicting interests in mind as you read this book. Think about how well different policies and court rulings promote one interest or the other. Judge for yourself how well the courts strike a balance between legitimate public interests and private individual rights.

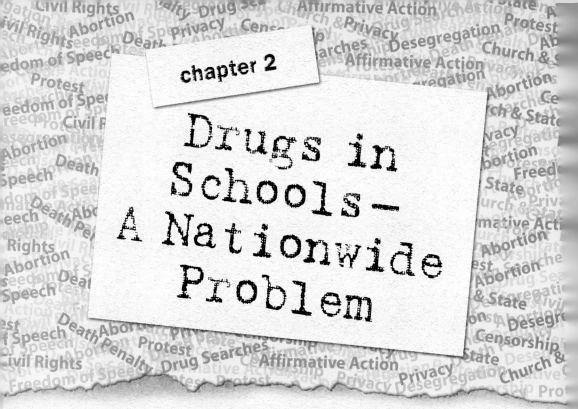

chapter 2

Drugs in Schools— A Nationwide Problem

Drugs and alcohol have serious health and safety effects that cause concern for schools and other government officials. What are some of those substances, and how does drug testing work?

Why Worry About Drugs and Alcohol?

"Don't do drugs" is a message schools start teaching very early. The reason is that drugs and alcohol cause serious health problems.

People who use drugs and alcohol often do so because the substances trigger particular feelings. That happens because the substances change how the brain produces and responds to chemicals that send messages to and from nerve cells. These chemicals, called neurotransmitters, also control essential body functions.

Over time, users can build up a tolerance to different drugs. In other words, people need more and more to get the same effect. That can lead to physical and emotional dependence. Once users become addicted, they need to continue using a drug, despite its adverse consequences. Addiction interferes substantially with people's ability to function normally. Eventually, getting and using the drug becomes the primary focus in an addicted person's life.

Children and teens are especially susceptible to drugs and alcohol. Research shows that early drug and alcohol use increases the chances of dependence problems later on.

Beyond this, the brain keeps maturing until about age twenty-one. Substance abuse interferes with that growth. Drug and alcohol use can also interfere with emotional development. Additionally, alcohol and drugs can make young people more likely to engage in risky behaviors.

Drugs and alcohol do not just affect the people who use them. They are a factor in a high percentage of violent crimes. Plus, they greatly increase the risks of serious accidents.

Tobacco does not dramatically change users' moods or coordination. However, it is a major cause of heart and lung disease, plus other illnesses. Nicotine in tobacco is very addictive. Schools worry about underage tobacco use, and the law forbids sales of tobacco to people under age eighteen. Thus, some testing programs look for tobacco use, even though it is generally not a crime to smoke tobacco.

Alcohol is legal for most adults to use. However, federal law forbids alcohol sales to people under age twenty-one. Various laws also make it a crime for teens to be under the influence of alcohol.

Alcohol is the most widely abused drug in the United States. Alcohol is a depressant, which means it slows or limits the body's reactions. Among other things, it causes mood changes, drowsiness, memory problems, coordination problems, and confusion.

Alcohol lowers users' inhibitions, or self-control. That impairs people's judgment and the ability to control impulses. Some users become very aggressive. Users may also become more likely to engage in other risky behaviors, such as sexual activity.

At very high levels, alcohol overdoses can lead to coma and death. Over time, heavy drinkers may also suffer liver damage, increased cancer risks, and circulatory disease.

Marijuana causes drastic mood swings in some people. Users also sometimes experience heightened sensations while using the drug.

Marijuana impairs people's ability to learn and remember things. Also, users' heart rates can zoom up to 160 beats per minute. Meanwhile, marijuana interferes with balance and control. Over time, users can also experience coughs and respiratory problems, just as cigarette smokers do.

Stimulants speed up the body's metabolism. Cocaine is an illegal stimulant that users often inhale in the form of a white powder. Crack is a smokable form of cocaine. Amphetamines often come in the form of pills. Methamphetamine in the form of crystals ("ice") or powder ("crank") is a very powerful amphetamine. Ecstasy, or MDMA (methylenedioxymethamphetamine), is a club drug that acts as both a stimulant and a hallucinogen.

Stimulants make users feel energetic. Yet users often become unable to concentrate. Many people who take stimulants grow anxious and aggressive. Meanwhile, the drugs tax the body's circulatory system, which can cause heart attacks. Over time, stimulants also cause sleep problems and impair memory and learning.

Depressants slow down the central nervous system. Among other things, the drugs often impair users' coordination, and overdoses can be fatal. Besides alcohol, the club drugs GHB (gamma hydroxybutyrate) and ketamine are depressants, along with the "date rape drug," Rohypnol. Various sedatives and tranquilizers are depressants too.

Opiates are a class of drugs derived from the poppy plant. They include heroin, morphine, and codeine. Synthetic versions also exist. Some opiate drugs have valuable uses as painkillers. However, when people use opiates to get "high," they are very addictive.

Hallucinogens interfere with users' perceptions of reality. Examples include LSD (lysergic acid diethylamide), mescaline or peyote (also called "magic mushrooms"), and PCP (phencyclidine, also called "angel dust"). Some stimulants, such as ecstasy and MDA (methylenedioxyamphetamine), also have hallucinogenic effects.

"Bad trips" from hallucinogens have caused cases of suicides and disturbing flashbacks. Other effects include higher heart rate and blood pressure, nausea, sleeplessness, and tremors.

Inhalants include substances such as glue, paint thinner, nail polish remover, and aerosol products. As the name implies, users inhale the substances to get high. However, their toxic ingredients can be deadly.

Anabolic steroids are drugs related to the male hormone testosterone. Athletes sometimes use them to build muscle more quickly and get an edge in competition. However, side effects include violent mood swings, withdrawal depression, acne, elevated cholesterol, higher risks of liver and kidney disease, and impotence and other sexual effects.

Other performance-enhancing drugs also have dangerous side effects. For example, human growth hormone and similar drugs can cause abnormal growth, joint problems, high blood pressure, and pituitary gland disorders. Other hormones can cause dangerous blood sugar swings or interfere with bone mass. Blood-doping chemicals can increase risks for strokes and convulsions.

Scary Statistics

If you think alcohol and drug abuse is rare, guess again. A 2005 report from the Substance Abuse and Mental Health Services Administration (SAMHSA) found that, depending on the region, between 6 and 11 percent of Americans over age twelve have an addiction or abuse problem serious enough to need treatment.[1] Substance abuse starts early.

A 2004 report from the Monitoring the Future Study, published by the University of

The club drug ecstasy has become one of the most popular drugs among teens. Its use can cause addiction and severe medical problems.

Michigan and the National Institute on Drug Abuse, found that about one third of all twelfth graders had been drunk within the past month. About 39 percent of all twelfth graders reported using an illicit drug within the past year. Marijuana was the most common illegal drug, although about 20 percent of twelfth graders said they had used other illicit drugs.[2]

Unfortunately, the 2005 SAMHSA report found that many teens are not getting help to deal with substance abuse problems. Every state has thousands of young people who should be getting treatment for alcohol or drug abuse but are not.[3] This is a terrible loss to society.

Schools and communities have other worries too. In 2003, more than 17,000 people died in alcohol-related motor vehicle crashes in the United States.[4] Alcohol was also a factor in about 275,000 motor vehicle injuries. That rate translates to someone being injured about every two minutes.[5] Marijuana and other drugs contribute to accidents too.

Alcohol and drugs also play a major role in crime. The U.S. Department of Justice reports that many prison inmates committed crimes while under the influence of, or while trying to obtain, illegal drugs.[6] MADD (Mothers Against Drunk Driving) also reports that alcohol plays a role in about 40 percent of violent crimes.[7]

How Drug Tests Work

Drug treatment facilities use drug testing routinely to make sure patients stick to their treatment programs. Law enforcement agencies use drug testing too. For example, police officers can ask someone suspected of drunk driving to take a Breathalyzer test to determine blood alcohol content. Likewise, some parolees from prison must submit to random drug tests to show that they are not using substances prohibited by the terms of their parole. Prisons also use tests to make sure inmates do not use forbidden substances.

In recent years, drug testing has branched out to cover many more people—and not just those who seem likely to use drugs. The U.S. military began drug testing for some soldiers in 1971. The program covered all personnel by the mid-1980s.[8] Also, in 1986, President Ronald Reagan ordered all federal agencies to have drug testing programs.

By the mid-1990s, almost half of America's thousand top moneymaking firms had some type of drug testing.[9] Private workplace drug testing aims to reduce accidents and limit legal liability. Employers also want to fulfill their duty to run a drug-free workplace. Unless the testing occurs under government-issued rules, the Fourth Amendment usually does not apply to private workplace drug testing.

Before the Supreme Court's 1995 decision in *Vernonia School District 47J* v. *Acton,* fewer than two dozen schools nationwide tested students for drugs. By 2002, the number had mushroomed to about one thousand programs.[10] After the 2002 decision in *Board of Education of Independent School District No. 92 of Pottawatomie County* v. *Earls,* more schools have added student drug testing programs. Tests have different degrees of accuracy, but all testing methods have limitations.

Blood tests. These measure the presence of various drugs in a sample. Because the test involves taking blood from a person, most people view it as more invasive than other types of tests. For this reason, schools have stayed away from blood tests in their drug testing programs.

Breath analysis. Breathalyzers measure the proportion of ethyl alcohol from a breath sample to calculate blood alcohol content. Breathalyzers and other tests can only tell if someone has used alcohol if the person takes the test before the body metabolizes (chemically breaks down) it. Men do this at a rate of about one drink per hour, while women usually take somewhat longer.[11]

Subject to certain limitations, many people feel Breathalyzers are reliable.[12] Indeed, drivers in some states can lose driving privileges for a period if they refuse to take a Breathalyzer test when police ask. Some schools use Breathalyzers at dances or other events.

Urinalysis. The drug testing programs in the *Earls* and *Vernonia* cases used urinalysis. Urine tests analyze samples for metabolites—chemicals left over after a person's body has processed certain drugs.

Tampering with urine samples can alter the results, so testing programs try to prevent that. At schools, adults are usually present in restrooms while students give samples. Monitors also check urine samples for color and temperature. Some medicines can alter test results, so programs also ask what medicines people are taking.

Urine tests' ability to detect different drugs varies. Tests may detect the use of cocaine and other amphetamines, as well as certain barbiturates and opiate drugs, for two to three days after someone uses the drugs. Urine tests for marijuana or PCP may be positive for about a week after use, although signs of long-term marijuana use may show for up to six weeks afterward.[13]

On the other hand, urine tests can detect alcohol use only for a few hours after consumption. Similarly, drug testing methods cannot reliably detect the use of inhalants. And tests detect only the drugs that schools ask labs to look for.

Programs can use different methods to analyze urine samples. For immunoassay tests, someone adds a small amount of a chemical to some urine. If the sample changes color, that shows the presence of a drug metabolite. At many schools, a nurse or other trained employee can usually do this test.

Thin-layer chromatography is another low-cost test. Different chemicals in a sample separate out by color. Distinctive patterns show use of certain drugs.

Among other things, these methods produce too many false positives. A false positive here means a result that says a drug is present when it really is not. Thus, in many testing programs, any samples that test positive with either method go on to a lab for more analysis.

Certified labs using Gas Chromatograph/Mass Spectrometry (GC/MS) report high degrees of accuracy. The lab used for the program in the *Vernonia* case claimed its procedures were 99.94 percent accurate in detecting amphetamines, cocaine, marijuana, and other drugs.[14]

Hair tests. These tests analyze hair samples for past use of drugs. Because hair needs time to grow, very recent use may not show up. However, signs of longer term drug use may last longer than they would with urine tests.

Handling and storing hair is easy. Plus, people may find giving a hair sample less offensive than urine testing. However, on-site personnel cannot screen samples the way they can with urine. Thus, testing costs tend to be higher because all samples must go to a lab. Results also may vary due to ethnic characteristics, hair color, length, and other factors.[15]

Some schools use Breathalyzers at school events to make sure participants have not been drinking. These students are about to attend a prom in Grant, Nebraska.

Oral fluid tests. Some drug testing programs do an analysis of oral fluids. A person rubs a swab between the lower cheek and gums for about two minutes. That collects saliva and other liquids in the mouth. The swab then goes to a lab for analysis.

Oral fluid tests may cause less embarrassment to students than urine tests. On the other hand, signs of different drugs' usage do not stay in oral fluids as long. Generally, they detect only very recent drug use.[16]

Sweat tests. For sweat tests, patches on the skin collect perspiration for up to a week. Labs then analyze the samples. The Office of National Drug Control Policy says the stigma of having to wear sweat patches makes them unsuitable for student drug testing.[17]

Drug Testing Costs

Costs for student drug testing programs vary widely. The choice of test method is a big factor. Urine tests, for example, tend to cost less than oral fluid screens or hair tests.

Also, the more substances a lab is looking for, the more testing is likely to cost. A limited drug test on a urine sample might cost $15, for example. However, testing urine samples for steroids could add over $100 per test.[18]

Costs per test are not the only numbers to consider. A random drug testing program might test only one fourth of the total students in sports and activities. However, the whole group could feel any effect that the program might have on preventing drug use. Arguably, then, the money spent would benefit the whole group.

Alternatively, one could look at how many students get counseling as a result of student drug tests. If the numbers were very low, the costs per pupil treated would be much higher than the per-test cost.

As the following chapters show, people who support student drug testing feel the costs are well spent. People who oppose student drug testing disagree.

chapter 3

Arguments for Student Drug Testing

People who favor student drug testing programs genuinely believe they help protect students from the dangers of drug abuse. President Bush summed up this feeling in his 2004 State of the Union Address: "The aim here is not to punish children, but to send them this message: We love you, and we don't want to lose you."[1]

Likewise, the Office of National Drug Control Policy maintains that schools with drug testing programs send "a message that local community leaders care enough to help those students showing warning signs of drug abuse and that they want to provide a drug-free learning environment to all students."[2] What other arguments support student drug testing programs?

Drug Testing Is Another Tool in the War Against Drugs

Schools have taught about the dangers of drugs for decades. And studies show gains in curbing teen drug use.[3] Yet drug abuse is still a substantial problem in America. Thus, some schools try student drug testing as yet another tool in the war against drugs. John Walters, director of National Drug Control Policy, explained:

> We know that random student drug testing is a powerful tool that school administrators can use to prevent young people from using drugs and identify those who may have a drug problem. The purpose of random testing is not to catch, punish, or expose students who use drugs, but to save their lives and discover abuse problems early so that students can grow up and learn in a drug-free environment.[4]

Is testing really a "powerful tool" for fighting drug abuse? One study published in 2003 compared two Oregon high schools. One school had a drug testing program for students who played sports. The other did not. As the 1999 school year started, drug use was generally similar for athletes at both schools.

By the end of the school year, the percentage of athletes who used alcohol, tobacco, or other drugs within the past month went from 33 to 31 percent for the school with drug testing. Use of illicit drugs that are illegal for everyone dropped from

7.4 to 5.3 percent. Usage rates for steroids and other performance-enhancing drugs went from 9.8 to 5.3 percent. Athletes' tobacco usage dropped too, from about 41 to 31 percent.

At the other school, the percentage of athletes using any drugs in the past month rose from 34 to 42 percent. The rate of illicit drug use nearly tripled, from 6.5 to 19.4 percent.[5] The study's authors concluded that random drug testing appears to lower substance abuse.

"More students in the school with drug testing reported using less drugs than those without a drug testing program," explains Linn Goldberg, the study's lead author.[6] However, not all the results were good news. There was no difference between the two high schools in the percentages of students who tried drugs for the first time. Researchers also did not find any significant change in athletes' drinking at the school with drug testing.

More seriously, athletes' attitudes about risky behavior and the consequences of drug use got worse at the school with drug testing. In theory, those views could put students at a greater risk for using drugs. Athletes' positive feelings about school suffered too.[7]

Another study surveyed eighty-three school principals in Indiana. Pending court challenges, their schools suspended student drug testing programs in 2000. Of the principals surveyed,

Lisa Brady, principal of a New Jersey high school, speaks in favor of drug testing in schools. Brady says that testing has reduced drug use in her school significantly.

85 percent noted a rise in drug or alcohol usage after the testing programs stopped. In a 2003 follow-up study, 73 percent of the principals saw drug usage go down when the programs started again in fall of 2002.[8] In yet another follow-up study in 2005, forty-nine out of fifty-four high school principals felt random drug testing in fact limited peer pressure to use drugs.[9]

Still another study looked at drug testing in nine schools. The schools generally experienced improved student behavior and increased productivity. Some schools also reported fewer fights, disciplinary referrals, and student arrests. However, one school in the study admitted that alcohol had "become the drug of choice among athletes" because it was accepted in the community and testing was not likely to detect it.[10]

Some case studies also say testing deters drug abuse. George Jenkins High School in Lakeland, Florida, saw drug use drop in the late 1990s after it started drug testing for athletes. When the program stopped in 2001 due to budget cuts, however, drug usage rates climbed back up. Using federal grant money, the school started drug testing again. Its 2004 tests turned up just two positive results for marijuana. School officials saw that as a sign that drug testing works.[11]

Hunterdon Central Regional High School in Flemington, New Jersey, also noted drops in drug use after it began random drug testing for student athletes. The number of tenth graders using little or no drugs or alcohol went up five percentage points. "We have never seen a prevention curriculum that affected the numbers this substantially," noted Principal Lisa Brady.[12]

However, not all studies are positive. A 2003 study at the University of Michigan, for example, found that drug testing programs did not make a significant difference in students' use of drugs.[13] More studies are under way.

Another Reason to Say No

Back in the 1980s, ads against drug abuse told young people, "Just say no." But as surveys showed, that was not enough to stop drug abuse. For many young people, a simple "no" was not enough to resist peer pressure.

Principal Lisa Brady felt her school's testing program gave students support for resisting peer pressure to use drugs. "Kids will tell you that the program gives them a reason to say no," said Brady.[14]

John Walters, the director of the Office of National Drug Control Policy, agrees. "I have visited several schools with drug testing programs," he wrote, "and I have found that random drug testing gives kids an excuse to say what they really want to say when offered drugs—'no.'"[15]

Drug testing programs may change the dynamics of peer pressure at a school. Students are not saying no because they are weak or wimpy. Rather, they can proudly say they play football, perform music, or take part in other activities. They can support each other in staying away from drugs. And, supporters say, because random testing can catch drug use, it is not worth the risk of using drugs.

Drug Testing Helps Schools Keep Students Safe

When parents send their children to school, they trust schools to teach their children well. Today a good education does not just consist of reading, writing, and arithmetic. It also includes health education, along with the knowledge and tools to help young people resist drugs.

Schools' responsibility also includes keeping children safe. Supporters say that drug testing promotes that goal. In their view, testing reduces substance abuse. Plus, it promotes safety in school activities.

For example, athletes under the influence of drugs or alcohol are more likely to hurt themselves and others. Other activities at school can also present risks, and drug use would increase the chances for accidents.

Drugs do not just harm the people who use them. Alcohol and other drugs increase the risks of violent behavior. Widespread substance abuse at a school can create an atmosphere of fear. It detracts from the educational setting as well. The Student Drug-Testing Coalition and other supporters of drug testing say schools have a responsibility to provide a safe, drug-free learning environment.

In a 2004 study in Indiana, high schools with student drug testing saw a 30 percent drop in suspensions for drugs, alcohol, and weapons. Students also reported feeling much safer on school grounds with drug testing programs in place.[16] Supporters of drug testing say results like this show programs promote student safety.

Drug Testing Gets Students the Help They Need

Supporters of drug testing insist the programs do not punish students. Rather, they find out which students need help. And they provide those counseling and other resources to help them beat addiction and other drug-related problems.

Caring parents talk to their children about drugs and watch for signs of abuse. Yet people who do drugs can be very clever at covering up their abuse. As a result, many parents do not find out about children's drug abuse until tragedy strikes. For school administrator Herbert Levine in Salem, Massachusetts, this concern trumps objections about student privacy. "Is the ACLU going to go to the funeral of the next kid on the North Shore who overdosed on OxyContin or heroin and say, 'Hey, I protected his privacy?'" he asked in an article in *The Boston Globe*.[17]

Testing Programs Are Worth the Cost

Getting students the help they need is well worth the costs, say supporters of drug testing. Moreover, those costs are reasonable and affordable, they say. In one 2005 survey, 91 percent of Indiana high schools with drug testing programs spent $30 or less per test. Seven of the fifty-four schools spent just $15 per test.[18]

While these costs can add up to tens of thousands of dollars per year, drug abuse has much larger costs. Drug abuse places added burdens on the health care system. It strains the criminal justice system. It causes property damage and lost productivity. And it takes a terrible toll on people and their families.

Random Drug Testing Makes Students Accountable

Schools expect students to study math, science, and other subjects. And they test students to make sure they are in fact learning their lessons. Supporters of drug testing see the programs as a way to make sure students are learning another important lesson—to stay away from drugs.

The law already imposes a duty on students not to use drugs. Additionally, school policies prohibit tobacco, alcohol, and other drugs on school property or at school functions. With limited exceptions, such as for asthma inhalers, students often cannot carry even legal medicines at school. Rather, they must see a school nurse or administrator.

Supporters say drug testing reinforces policies the school already has in effect. As one Indiana case noted, drug testing is another way school officials can make sure that students obey the rules for off-campus activities.[19] Drug testing also underscores the importance of staying drug-free. As Indiana high school student Kyle Brown argued, it "gives teeth to the drug-free promise" athletes and students in extracurricular activities make anyway.[20]

For many supporters, random drug testing is better than testing based on individualized suspicion. Just as parents cannot always tell if their children are using drugs, teachers and school officials cannot spot all problems either. Moreover, it is not always clear when a school official would have sufficient suspicion on a case-by-case basis.

Random sampling or blanket testing programs also reduce worries that schools might use testing to pick on unpopular students. Supporters feel random testing programs involve less shame, because there is no accusation of wrongdoing when students are asked to give samples.

Yes, random or blanket testing involves some students whom no one suspects of using drugs. However, all students have a duty to stay away from drugs anyway. As one Oklahoma parent put it, "If you don't take them, you don't have anything to worry about."[21]

Drug Testing Is a Negligible Intrusion on Student Privacy

Students already have to comply with various health requirements. States require various vaccinations. Most students also need doctors' exams to take part in different programs. Supporters of drug testing programs feel any added intrusion on student privacy is negligible.

Indeed, students who take part in sports and various other programs already change clothes or shower with other students around. Likewise, school restrooms usually have space for multiple students. Students using those facilities can expect that other people will be nearby to see or hear what they do.

In that atmosphere, supporters of drug testing say, collecting urine samples with adult monitors present poses little added burden. Indeed, drug testing monitors often show more respect for students' privacy than they get when showering after gym class. Oral fluid testing or hair sampling poses even less potential for embarrassment. Supporters feel those methods could virtually eliminate concerns about privacy.

Beyond this, schools have written procedures for confidentiality. Often labs do not know the names of students whose samples they analyze. Likewise, schools are supposed to give confidential treatment to data about students' prescriptions and medical conditions. After the labs finish their analysis, only a few school officials have access to the results.

Moreover, drug testing policies clearly limit schools' use of test results. If students test positive for drugs, policies generally call for schools to notify the students and their parents. Policies also generally let students take a second test or show why a false positive may have occurred. Many schools also keep data on individuals' drug testing results separate from their general school records.

Ultimately, the constitutional test for what the government can do in a search and seizure comes down to reasonableness. Supporters of drug testing say the programs are very reasonable. In their view, the potential positive results far outweigh any small inconvenience to students.

chapter 4

Arguments Against Student Drug Testing

Opponents of student drug testing feel it violates young people's privacy rights. In addition, they challenge the wisdom and effectiveness of student drug testing.

Student Drug Testing Goes Against Traditional Fourth Amendment Standards

Critics like the American Civil Liberties Union and the Drug Policy Alliance say student drug testing turns the Fourth Amendment on its head. In their view, it goes against fundamental notions of individual liberty and privacy.

Random drug testing treats students as if they are guilty until proven innocent. Most students in school testing programs have done nothing wrong.

Yet they must give up private bodily fluids. Programs force students to give evidence to the government.

Plus, say critics, students bear the burden for explaining false positives. And if they refuse to take part in drug testing, they cannot take part in sports or other activities. Critics say that is clearly a punishment.

Admittedly, courts allow some government searches without a warrant when it is not practical to get one. Likewise, courts have allowed suspicionless searches—searches when there is no suspicion that the person has done anything wrong—in cases of overriding safety needs. A train conductor or bus driver using drugs, for example, could endanger innocent passengers. Likewise, armed law enforcement officers could put people in danger if they used drugs. School drug testing does not present the same urgency, opponents claim.

Critics also disagree that schools' special status lets them ride roughshod over student privacy rights. As the Supreme Court has said, children do not "shed their constitutional rights . . . at the schoolhouse gate."[1] Schools have a duty to educate children and provide a safe learning environment. But they should respect students' constitutional rights.

Schools already have effective tools to fight drug abuse and maintain order, say critics. School policies prohibit drugs at school and school events. Rules also forbid students from being under the influence of drugs at school and school functions. And if students act violently or commit crimes on campus, schools can discipline them, regardless of whether they have used drugs.

These steps may not catch drug abuse as easily as regular, random drug testing might. But the Fourth Amendment's goal is to protect privacy, not to promote efficiency. Critics like Justice Sandra Day O'Connor say that schools can deal with drug problems without widespread violations of students' privacy.[2] Also, student drug testing does not detect only substances used at school or at school events. For example, a urine test on Monday would probably detect marijuana used over the weekend. Critics say this wrongly expands schools' control over teens' private lives.

Random Drug Testing Is a Substantial Invasion of Privacy

Court decisions allowing school drug testing are "both foolhardy and dangerous," warns Judy Appel, deputy legal director for the Drug Policy Alliance. In her view, they send "exactly the wrong message to America's children—that they have no right to privacy."[3]

It is one thing to provide a urine sample for a family doctor whom the student trusts. Plus, no one listens outside a stall or watches from behind. It is another thing entirely to make students provide samples so schools can see if they did something wrong.

Moreover, critics say, school drug testing can be stressful. The adult to whom students hand their samples is often a well-known teacher or other authority figure, who may ask embarrassing questions about the sample.

While people may happen to overhear other people using a public restroom, that's different from knowing someone is deliberately listening. Also, some people feel awkward being asked to urinate on demand. In one Colorado case, a marching band member "tried five, six, seven times" to produce a sample, but he could not.[4]

Oral fluid tests and hair testing are less awkward and embarrassing than urine sampling. However, those methods still make students give up something from their bodies that schools will use to see if they have been taking drugs. In other words, students may still feel humiliated by being forced to give physical evidence that could be used against them.

Depending on how schools choose test subjects, other pupils may know who got tested. That can further embarrass teens.

Students may also feel awkward telling about prescription medications and other medical conditions. Schools typically require such information when students need to carry or take medicines during school hours. And parents sometimes tell schools about medicines students take on an ongoing basis.

However, there is no general obligation for parents to tell schools about antibiotics, antifungal medicines, or other legal drugs taken at home to cure temporary infections. In addition, worry about negative treatment, or stigma, could make parents or students want to withhold information about some medicines, such as those for psychiatric conditions.

Students may also resist telling schools about birth control pills or medicines to treat sexually transmitted diseases. In many cases, teens can legally get those drugs without parental consent. When school drug testing programs make students tell about such medicines, however, that works against the policy of encouraging them to get certain kinds of medical treatment.

Schools are supposed to protect against disclosure of confidential information. However, mistakes do occur. Another fear is that someone might use urine samples for other purposes, despite what policies say.

Supporters of drug testing downplay these concerns, but critics say that they are very real. Indeed, if the interests are really so minimal, why don't the courts let schools just require all students to go through drug testing? Why not make all adults in town submit to random drug tests, for that matter? Critics feel the answers are obvious. Significant privacy interests are at stake.

School Drug Testing Does Not Work

Critics of school drug testing say there is not sufficient scientific evidence to show that such programs stop or prevent drug abuse. A 2003 report by researchers at the University of Michigan studied national data on teen drug use and school drug testing. The researchers found no link between school drug testing and reported rates of illegal drug use among teens.[5]

Urine testing cannot reliably detect all drugs that students might use. Students sometimes switch from one substance to another to avoid detection. Also, detection periods for different drugs vary.

Indeed, alcohol is the most commonly used drug of abuse. Yet urine tests can reliably detect it only within several hours of use. With such a gaping hole in the tests' effectiveness, critics say school drug testing fails to deal with the most pressing problem of substance abuse.

Critics worry that students may switch to other dangerous drugs too, in order to get around drug testing programs. No standard test can detect inhalant abuse, for example. And not all tests scan for ecstasy or GHB. Yet those drugs can be lethal.

Critics say school drug testing really cannot stop substance abuse among young people. Policies make it sound as if schools are addressing drug abuse problems. But such programs are more for show than substance, opponents claim.

Drug Testing Wastes Schools' Scarce Resources

Critics also say the costs do not justify student drug testing. In Dublin, Ohio, only 11 out of 1,473 students tested positive for drugs during the school's random drug testing program. Yet the program's yearly cost was about $35,000. Deciding that it was not an efficient use of money, the school district ended the program.[6]

The Janesville School Board in Wisconsin voted to end its drug testing program too. Testing cost about $20,000 per year. But the program gave positive test results for fewer than ten students annually at each high school. "In a time when you're cutting programs and personnel and looking at reducing important services to students, we wanted to look at education or alternatives to drug testing," board member Mike Rundle said.[7]

Additionally, according to the Drug Policy Alliance and the American Civil Liberties Union, drug testing can drain resources needed for more effective programs to prevent substance abuse:

> The cost of drug testing sometimes exceeds the total a school district spends on existing drug education, prevention, and counseling programs. In fact, drug testing may actually take scarce resources away from the health and treatment services necessary for students who are misusing drugs—seriously undermining the original purpose of the drug test.[8]

Critics say the money spent on student drug testing would be better spent on other things. Schools could pursue more effective drug education programs. In their view, schools should not waste scarce resources on ineffective testing programs that interfere with student rights.

Drug Testing Should Not Deny Anyone a Quality Education

In America all children are entitled to a free public school education. In the twenty-first century, athletics and other school activities are an important part of the school experience. Indeed, many people feel that extracurricular activities are essential if students want to go to a good college.

Almost all of America's high schools offer such activities, and many school districts offer activities for students in the lower grades too. It is no wonder that about 80 percent of high school seniors take part in at least one such activity at their school.[9]

Yet student drug testing programs make the full benefits of a public school education depend upon consent to drug testing. Critics say this is wrong. As federal judge Kenneth Ripple wrote in one case that preceded *Earls*: "The case has yet to be made that a urine sample can be the 'tuition' at a public school."[10]

The government cannot condition one right upon giving up another. Yet critics say that is exactly what happens when the right to a quality public education depends on a student's willingness to give up the right to be free from random drug testing.

That pressure causes many parents to "consent" too, even when they feel drug testing is wrong for their children. "They took away the parents' job in the home," Lindsay Earls's mother said.[11]

Student drug testing could well be counterproductive, according to opponents. In one study, tenth graders who took part in no school activities were 49 percent more likely than other students to have used drugs.[12] Students who use drugs may be less likely to get involved in activities in the first place. Or school activities may help protect students against drug use. Either way, drug testing adds a barrier that could keep people out of clubs or sports.

Opponents of drug testing in schools argue that students who participate in activities, such as the orchestra, are already at lower risk of using drugs.

For these reasons, the American Academy of Pediatrics, the National Education Association, the American Public Health Association, the National Council on Alcoholism and Drug Dependence, and other groups went on record against school drug testing in the Earls case.[13] Among other things, their *amici curiae* ("friends of the court") brief stressed that school activities are an important "protective factor" in deterring drug use. Yet school drug testing could discourage students from taking part in those activities.

Meanwhile, the drug testing policy would do little for children who really did have substance abuse problems.[14]

While school drug testing may catch a few students using drugs, critics say, such programs foster resentment and distrust among students. That can poison the learning environment. As a 2004 bill that would have banned random drug testing in California stated: "Random, suspicion-less drug testing impairs the trust and cooperation between parents, pupils and school staff . . ., thereby distracting [all] from the core educational mission of the public schools."[15]

No Logical Limits

If random drug testing for all students in school activities is okay, where should the courts draw the line? Why not require drug testing for all students in high school? For that matter, why not take testing down to the kindergarten grade level? And why not require testing for other conditions too, such as sexually transmitted diseases?

Critics of school drug testing would oppose all these proposals. Yet the point is that the courts have not set out logical limits for what is and is not allowable under the Fourth Amendment. Reasonableness under this amendment calls for consideration of the facts and a balancing of costs and benefits. Yet if the courts presume that student drug testing is reasonable, when would students' privacy rights ever kick in?

Yes, foes of drug testing say, schools have a duty to teach children about the dangers of drugs. Yet schools should teach children to be good citizens and to stand up for important constitutional rights. As part of the government, schools teach by example. If they trample on individual rights, though, schools fail in that duty. Instead of learning to be good citizens, young people will see important government principles as "mere platitudes"—words with no real meaning.[16]

chapter 5

The Legal Context of Student Drug Testing

So far, drug testing in schools is mostly a matter of local law. However, national laws affect local drug testing policies, especially to the extent that they provide funds for such programs. Also, because school drug testing is a type of search and seizure, Fourth Amendment concerns enter in.

Adopting Drug Testing Policies

Public school education in the United States is largely the domain of local governments. School boards elected by cities, counties, or independent school districts have direct control over what goes on in public elementary, middle, and high schools. They set general policy for the public schools. They hire and fire teachers, administrators, and other staff. They also oversee public schools' financial matters.

In the absence of other sources, local taxes pay for public schools' costs for all programs. Local governments deal with assessments and collect taxes and decide how to spend that money. Spending money on any one program generally means that it is not available for other uses in the schools.

State and federal laws affect schools too. For example, state law sets curriculum standards. Federal and state laws forbid various types of discrimination. They require schools to maintain confidentiality of various student records. They restrict the types of discipline that schools are allowed to administer. They also call for schools to report data about students and to inform other government agencies about various incidents that could affect student safety.

A 2005 New Jersey law set up a statewide framework for student drug testing in the state's schools. Basically, the law outlines how programs should work, and it allows testing of students in school activities or with parking permits at school. The law should provide some uniformity across the state among schools that do testing. However, individual school districts must still decide whether they want student drug testing. They are not required to have it.[1] Other states may pass similar laws.

A few policy makers would like a nationwide requirement for random drug testing in schools. In 1999, for example, Representatives Jim Rogan (R-Calif.) and John Peterson (R-Penn.) introduced bills that would have required drug testing for all high school students with parental consent.[2] Neither of those bills passed.

In 2002, a federal education law made money available for local school districts to conduct student drug testing.[3] Starting in fiscal year 2003, the Department of Education began making such grants as part of its Safe and Drug-Free Schools Program. (In the federal government, a fiscal year is the period covered by the annual budget. Fiscal year 2003 started on October 1, 2002, and ended on September 30, 2003.)

During the program's first two years, seventy-nine schools used about $2 million in grants to get their testing programs under way. For fiscal year 2006 (October 1, 2005, to September 30, 2006), Congress approved over $10 million for student drug testing programs.[4] The President's budget for fiscal year 2007 asked for an increase to $15 million.[5] This suggests that the grant program may keep growing.

To qualify for those grants, schools must have a comprehensive drug education program. Among other things, they must provide referrals for counseling and treatment if testing identifies students as drug users. Plus, drug testing programs must be consistent with the programs approved by the Supreme Court in the *Vernonia* and *Earls* cases.[6]

Of course, school districts do not need a federal grant to do drug testing. They can pay with their own tax monies or get state grants. Sometimes businesses or nonprofit groups contribute too. Except for such private contributions, the money ultimately comes from taxpayers.

Government Searches Under the Fourth Amendment

The Fourth Amendment generally requires the government to have a warrant before searching any persons and their property. Its goal is to protect people's legitimate privacy expectations. Over the years, however, the courts have made various exceptions to that rule.

For example, a Supreme Court decision in 1968 said that police officers do not violate the Fourth Amendment when they stop and frisk people who act suspiciously and who may be committing a crime.[7] Exceptions also apply if police see evidence of a crime in plain sight.

Most searches and seizures require the government to have some grounds for suspecting possible wrongdoing. Again, however, the courts have made exceptions. In 1976, for example, the Supreme Court approved brief border searches by

Legal Terms

***amicus curiae* (plural, *amici curiae*)**—Literally, "friend of the court"; someone who files a brief in a case in which that person is not a party but has a strong interest. Such briefs let the court benefit from the added viewpoint.

appellate court (sometimes called a court of appeals)—A court that reviews decisions of lower courts for fairness and accuracy. An appellate court can reverse a lower court's ruling.

appellant or petitioner—The person who thinks the lower court made an error.

appellee or respondent—The person who won the case in the lower court.

brief—Written statement of a party's argument on one or more issues in the case.

concur—To agree with the ruling in a court case.

dissent—To disagree with the ruling in a court case.

majority opinion—The ruling and reasoning supported by a majority of appellate court judges in a case. **Concurring opinions** are written by judges who agree with the majority holding but have other reasons for their views. **Dissenting opinions** are written by judges who disagree with the ruling.

***per se*—**As such; by itself.

precedent—A legal holding that will determine how courts decide future cases.

customs agents.[8] While there was some small intrusion on privacy, the government had a right to protect its borders. Besides, without stopping everyone, there was no practical alternative. Similar reasoning supports the constitutionality of routine security screening for airline travelers.

Unless a search falls within an exception, the Fourth Amendment generally forbids it. A 1969 case on freedom of speech and expression gave us the rule that the Constitution's protections are not for adults only. In that case, the Court held that an Iowa school violated students' rights when it would not let them wear black armbands to school. The armbands were a sign of protest against the Vietnam War.[9]

In a similar vein, court decisions have held that the Fourth Amendment protects public school students from unlimited searches and seizures. However, that protection does not extend as far in the school setting as it does outside of school and for adults. The Supreme Court made this clear in 1985 in the case of *New Jersey* v. *T.L.O.*[10]

T.L.O. was a fourteen-year-old freshman at a New Jersey high school who was accused of smoking in the lavatory. The assistant principal searched her purse. Inside, he found marijuana, money, and evidence that T.L.O. was selling marijuana to other students. Afterward, T.L.O. faced charges in juvenile court. T.L.O.'s lawyers tried to keep the evidence out of court. The Supreme Court ruled that there was no violation of her constitutional rights.

The Court's majority opinion stressed that schools need to maintain discipline among students. They could not accomplish that goal, however, if every search and seizure had to meet the requirements imposed on the police for dealing with citizens in general. Justice Byron White wrote:

> It is evident that the school setting requires some easing of the restrictions to which searches by public authorities are ordinarily subject. The warrant requirement, in particular, is unsuited to the school environment: requiring a teacher to obtain a warrant before searching a child suspected of an infraction of school rules (or of the criminal law) would unduly interfere with the maintenance of the swift and informal disciplinary procedures needed in the schools.[11]

The Court also let a lower level of suspicion justify a search of students' belongings. Police generally need "probable cause" to do a search. Generally, this means that the sum of available and trustworthy information should be enough to lead a reasonably careful person to believe that evidence of a crime is present, or that a crime has been or is about to be committed. However, the majority felt such a strict standard should not apply at school. "The fundamental command of the Fourth Amendment is that searches and seizures be reasonable," Justice White wrote.[12]

To determine reasonableness, the Court looked at students' legitimate expectations of privacy in the school setting. Then the Court balanced that interest against the government need for a safe and productive school learning environment. The majority found that the search of T.L.O.'s purse was reasonable. Thus, the school had not violated her Fourth Amendment rights.

A trained dog searches for illegal drugs in lockers at a middle school. According to the Supreme Court, many searches of student belongings at schools are legal.

Justices John Paul Stevens, Thurgood Marshall, and William Brennan disagreed. Justice Stevens warned:

> The rule the Court adopts today is so open-ended that it may make the Fourth Amendment virtually meaningless in the school context. Although I agree that school administrators must have broad latitude to maintain order and discipline in our classrooms, that authority is not unlimited. . . .[13]

Since *New Jersey* v. *T.L.O.,* schools have become even more active in trying to stop drug use and violence. Some use metal detectors to stop people from bringing guns or knives into school. Others have drug-sniffing dogs come in to detect drugs in lockers or among the student body.

From a legal viewpoint, one rationale is that the special need to run a safe school justifies the general, noninvasive screening. A stronger argument is that the metal detectors or dogs are tools that schools can choose to have in their environment. When they sound an alarm, then schools have grounds to suspect particular students of wrongdoing. Schools' follow-up searches of students and their belongings are thus based on individualized suspicion.[14]

Student drug testing programs stem from a similar concern. By taking something from students' bodies without prior suspicion, however, it expands the government's authority to conduct searches and seizures at public schools. The next chapters show how the Supreme Court has dealt with this issue.

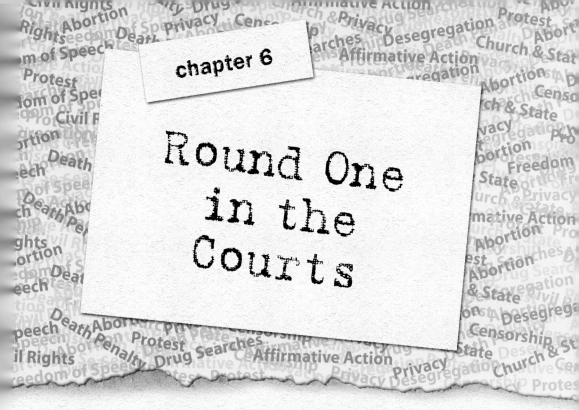

chapter 6

Round One in the Courts

Drug testing first came before the Supreme Court in two 1989 cases dealing with the workplace. In both cases, the Supreme Court agreed that the Fourth Amendment applied to drug testing because of government action. However, most members of the Court were willing to make exceptions for "special needs." Because those cases set the stage for challenges to drug testing in schools, it is important to look at the Court's reasoning.

Drug Testing in the Workplace

The issue came before the Supreme Court in two 1989 cases. In both cases, the Court upheld the use of drug and alcohol testing in the workplace.

Skinner v. *Railway Labor Executives' Assn.* The issue in this case was drug and alcohol testing in the railway industry. Federal rules required railways to conduct blood and urine tests when employees were involved in train accidents. The rules also called for drug and alcohol tests if workers broke various safety rules.

The Supreme Court held that the required drug testing was a search and seizure under the Fourth Amendment. However, it did not violate workers' constitutional rights.

Justice Anthony Kennedy wrote the majority opinion, which Justices William Rehnquist, Byron White, Harry Blackmun, Sandra Day O'Connor, and Antonin Scalia joined.[1] In the majority's view, "special needs" justified doing the drug and alcohol tests without warrants.

Specifically, railway safety is an important public interest, and drug and alcohol use on the job is dangerous. Also, getting a warrant right after a railway accident would be impractical.

Justice John Paul Stevens concurred in, or agreed with, the result. However, he questioned whether drug testing would actually deter drug and alcohol use. If the fear of serious railway accidents did not keep workers from using drugs, what could testing add?

Justices Thurgood Marshall and William Brennan dissented. They felt the drug testing wrongly invaded workers' privacy rights under the Fourth Amendment. "The majority's acceptance of dragnet blood and urine testing ensures that the first, and worse, casualty of the war on drugs will be the precious liberties of our citizens," warned Justice Marshall.[2]

Treasury Employees v. *Von Raab.* This case took workplace drug testing a step further. The Court upheld drug testing for all customs agents who might intercept illegal drugs or whose jobs let them carry a gun. The customs department was "largely drug-free." Yet the Court again held that special needs justified the drug tests.

The government has "a compelling interest" in making sure that the frontline people in the war against drugs are fit and have excellent character, Justice Kennedy wrote in the majority opinion.[3] Likewise, drug users should not get government jobs where they carry guns. Justices Rehnquist, White, Blackmun, and O'Connor joined in Justice Kennedy's opinion.

As in *Skinner,* Justices Marshall and Brennan dissented. This time, though, Justices Scalia and Stevens dissented too.

"I think it obvious that it is a type of search particularly destructive of privacy and offensive to personal dignity," wrote Justice Scalia.[4] The customs department did not have significant drug use problems. Therefore, testing would not prevent any real danger to the public.

Schools Start Testing

Meanwhile, a few school districts had started random drug testing for students. In *Schaill* v. *Tippecanoe County School Corp.*, the Seventh Circuit Court of Appeals upheld a urine drug testing program for student athletes.[5] That 1988 decision bound all federal courts in Illinois, Indiana, and Wisconsin. In 1991, however, the Fifth Circuit Court of Appeals rejected a Texas school district's random drug testing program for everyone in school activities. That case, *Brooks* v. *East Chambers Consol. Independent School District*, bound all federal courts in Texas, Louisiana, and Mississippi.[6]

The drug testing programs in *Schaill* and *Brooks* differed in scope, so the court decisions did not directly contradict each other. Then the Ninth Circuit Court of Appeals—covering nine western states—held that an Oregon testing program for student athletes was unconstitutional. Now two federal courts of appeal had conflicting rulings for basically the same situation. The Supreme Court agreed to hear the case.

Vernonia School District 47J v. Acton

Starting in the middle to late 1980s, school officials in Vernonia, Oregon, saw a "sharp increase in drug use." Student attitudes also seemed to shift in favor of the drug culture. Meanwhile, student discipline problems grew to "epidemic proportions."[7]

The school district held special classes and programs. It even used a trained dog to sniff out drugs at school. However, the drug problem continued.

In 1989, the district began drug testing for all students in interscholastic sports. Parents who came to a planning meeting about the proposed policy all approved of it. In order to play, students and their parents had to consent in writing to the drug testing program. All athletes had to give a urine sample at the start of the sports season. Each week afterward, a random drawing selected 10 percent of the athletes for additional testing.

An independent lab screened all samples for amphetamines, cocaine, and marijuana. The district could also ask the lab to test for other drugs, such as LSD. The testing lab claimed that its analyses were 99.94 percent accurate. Only the superintendent, the principals, vice-principals, and athletic directors got information about students' identities and test results.

If someone tested positive for a drug, he or she would submit another urine sample. Only if the second test was also positive would the district notify the athlete's parents. The student would then take part in an intervention program with weekly urine drug tests. If the student refused, or if it was a second offense, the district would suspend the student from sports for the rest of that season and the next one. A third offense would result in suspension for the current season, plus the next two athletic seasons. However, drug testing results would not lead to criminal action. Nor would they result in suspension or expulsion from school.

James Acton was a seventh grader who wanted to play on his school's football team. However, James and his parents refused to allow the random drug testing. Thus, James could not play football.

As James saw it, he was "one of the smartest kids in the class." He was an A student and did not have discipline problems. James felt that should have been "proof enough" that he was not using drugs.[8] With help from the American Civil Liberties Union, the Actons sued in federal court. Among other things, they claimed the drug testing violated the Fourth and Fourteenth Amendments to the U.S. Constitution.

During oral argument, Justice Sandra Day O'Connor asked why the school did not just test students whom coaches suspected of using drugs. The school's lawyer argued that a serious drug problem in the schools justified the random testing of all athletes. But if that were so, Justice David Souter asked, "Haven't you in fact made a case for random testing of the entire student population in these schools?"

James Acton, a seventh grader, believed he should not have to be tested for drugs in order to play interscholastic sports at his Oregon school. Here he and his attorney, Thomas M. Christ, speak with reporters outside the Supreme Court.

"A significant difference," Justice Ruth Bader Ginsburg noted, was that all children must go to school. However, athletes choose to play sports. Thus, they have some choice.

The school's lawyer added that athletes had led the group causing problems because of drugs. "How do they know that if they don't have individualized suspicion?" asked Justice John Paul Stevens. The question challenged the argument that the school needed random testing to find out who used drugs.

Other questions dealt with the question of privacy interests. "Well, how much privacy is there in a boy's locker room with a bunch of urinals lined up against the wall, [and] guys walking naked from the shower to the lockers?" asked Chief Justice William Rehnquist. Likewise, Justice Stephen Breyer noted that people urinate in restrooms all over the country. "It isn't really a tremendously private thing, is it?" Breyer asked.

Meanwhile, Justice Antonin Scalia focused on the school setting. "But you're dealing with children," he told the Actons' lawyer. "You're not dealing with adults who have a totally different set of rights."[9]

Ultimately, the Court upheld the district's drug testing program. Justice Scalia wrote the majority opinion. Justices Rehnquist, Breyer, Kennedy, Thomas, and Ginsburg joined in.

The opinion stated that the drug testing program was a search subject to the Fourth Amendment.

However, Justice Scalia stressed, "the ultimate measure of the constitutionality of a governmental search is 'reasonableness.'"[10] In the majority's view, the district's drug testing program passed muster.

First, the Court's opinion noted basic limits on children's rights. Children are subject "to the control of their parents or guardians." When parents send them to school, the schools are "*in loco parentis* over the children entrusted to them." This means that the school is temporarily in the place of the parent. The U.S. Constitution imposes some limits. Nonetheless, the Court said, schools have "a degree of supervision and control that could not be exercised over free adults."[11]

For example, schools require vaccinations and health screenings. Some people might object. However, the requirements protect the general well-being of the school community.

"Legitimate privacy expectations are even less with regard to student athletes," wrote Justice Scalia. He explained:

> School sports are not for the bashful. They require "suiting up" before each practice or event, and showering and changing afterwards. Public school locker rooms, the usual sites for these activities, are not notable for the privacy they afford. . . .[12]

Additionally, student athletes agree to added regulations when they sign up for sports. They must get physical exams. They need adequate insurance. They have to maintain minimum grade point averages. And they must obey rules set by the coach and athletic director. As Justice Scalia saw it,

> Somewhat like adults who choose to participate in a "closely regulated industry," students who voluntarily participate in school athletics have reason to expect intrusions upon normal rights and privileges, including privacy.[13]

The Court also downplayed the invasive nature of the drug testing. Boys stayed fully clothed and faced away from an adult male monitor as they filled sample cups. Girls went into stalls while a female monitor stood outside. In the majority's view, that was a "negligible" intrusion on students' privacy. Likewise, the Court found no problem with students having to tell up front what pre-scription medicines they took.

In contrast, the Court found that the testing served a "compelling state interest," meaning "an interest that appears *important enough* to justify the particular search at hand." That interest was "deterring drug use by our Nation's school-children" during their most vulnerable years. The opinion continued:

> And of course the effects of a drug-infested school are visited not just upon the users, but upon the entire student body and faculty, as the educational process is disrupted. In the present case, moreover, the necessity for the State to act is magnified by the fact that this evil is being visited not just upon individuals at large, but upon

children for whom it has undertaken a special responsibility of care and direction.[14]

Furthermore, the Court noted, the district's policy was narrow in scope. It covered only student athletes. Those students served as role models, yet the district felt they were often leaders of the drug problem. Plus, evidence showed a higher risk of injury if athletes used drugs. Thus, it was "self-evident" that the program dealt with the problem at hand.

The majority of the Court also rejected the idea that the school district should test only those suspected of using drugs. In that case, students might see drug testing as a "badge of shame." More generally, wrote Justice Scalia, the Fourth Amendment does not require the "least intrusive" search that is practical.[15]

Justice Ginsburg's one-paragraph concurring opinion went along with upholding the drug testing program for athletes. She reserved judgment on whether a school could constitutionally require routine drug testing for everyone.[16]

The Dissenting Views in *Vernonia*

Justice Sandra Day O'Connor dissented from the majority view, along with Justices John Paul Stevens and David Souter. Broad, suspicionless testing programs could involve thousands or even millions of searches. In the dissenters' view, that presented "a greater threat to liberty" than searches based on individual suspicion. Suspicion-based searches usually affect only one person at a time. Plus, people can often avoid them by not acting suspiciously in the first place.

"For most of our constitutional history, mass, suspicionless searches have been generally considered *per se* unreasonable within the meaning of the Fourth Amendment," stressed Justice O'Connor.[17] During colonial times, British officials often used general writs of assistance to search homes for anything and everything that might show wrongdoing. To prevent such abuse, the Fourth Amendment required both individualized suspicion and objective probable cause. "Protection of privacy, not evenhandedness, was then and is now the touchstone of the Fourth Amendment," wrote Justice O'Connor.[18]

Citing Justice Scalia's dissent in the *Treasury Employees* case, Justice O'Connor argued that "state-compelled, state-monitored collection and testing of urine . . . is still 'particularly destructive of privacy and offensive to personal dignity.'"[19] Indeed, other less intrusive searches got Fourth Amendment protection. One case, for example, limited the government's ability to scrape under someone's fingernails for dirt.[20]

While the Supreme Court had allowed drug testing for closely regulated industries, requiring suspicion each time would not have prevented substantial harm in those cases. In contrast, the Vernonia schools had effective ways to handle discipline problems. Plus, school officials could often spot likely drug users. Drug testing only for such suspicious cases would be "*significantly* less intrusive," Justice O'Connor believed.[21]

In any case, problems at the high school did not justify drug testing at James Acton's grade school. In Justice O'Connor's view, "Testing all student-athletes sweeps too broadly, and too imprecisely, to be reasonable under the Fourth Amendment."[22]

After *New Jersey* v. *T.L.O.,* schools no longer needed warrants and probable cause to search students or their property.[23] By doing away with the need for individual suspicion, random drug testing seemed to get rid of any Fourth Amendment protection for students, the dissent said.

The decision in *Vernonia School District* v. *Acton* made national news. Soon, more school districts started student drug testing programs. That led to more litigation.

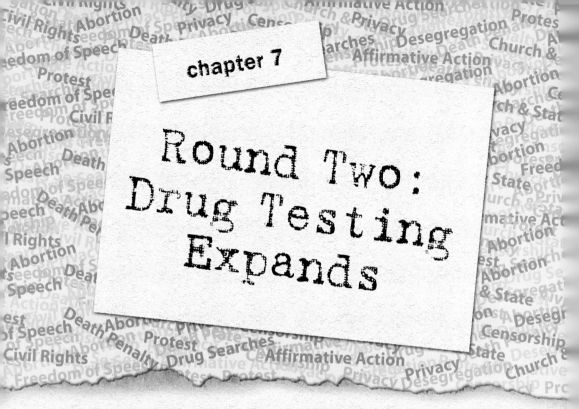

chapter 7

Round Two: Drug Testing Expands

The Supreme Court in the *Vernonia* case allowed drug testing for student athletes. Yet it said that suspicionless drug testing would not necessarily be all right in other contexts. Thus, in 1997, the Court overturned a Georgia law that required drug testing for all candidates for state office.[1] The government's symbolic interest in taking a stand against drug use was not a special need that outweighed individuals' legitimate privacy expectations.

A 2001 Supreme Court case even overturned a suspicion-based drug testing program. *Ferguson* v. *City of Charleston* held that a public hospital could not test pregnant women for suspected cocaine use without their consent.[2]

On the other hand, federal appeals courts upheld random drug testing for school teachers or other school employees.[3] Another case upheld random drug testing for employees who regularly went into the Old Executive Office Building in Washington, D.C., where many White House staffers work.[4] Yet another case found that drug testing for firefighters passed constitutional muster.[5] Each case seemed to turn on how well the government proved that there was a special need for the testing.

Meanwhile, hundreds of school boards across the country took their cue from the *Vernonia* case and began drug testing programs. Some schools' testing programs were like that in the *Vernonia* school district, focusing on athletes only. Other programs were much broader.

Focus on Extracurricular Activities

In the *Vernonia* case, the Supreme Court said that testing student athletes for drugs was all right. Yet many of the reasons for doing drug testing could apply to almost any extracurricular activity. Weren't there also role models for other pupils in student council, band, chorus, and other clubs? And if students in those groups used drugs, wouldn't that add to discipline problems? Plus, drugs can harm any student in a school club—not just those in sports.

Besides, the broader a drug testing program was, the more likely it could be to catch anyone using drugs. Schools might not yet be able to test every student at school for drugs. But some schools wanted to test as many students as possible.

Thus, some drug testing policies covered all students in any extracurricular activities. Submitting to random urine tests got added to any other conditions for joining school clubs. Besides, school boards reasoned, they were not forcing students to submit to drug tests. Students always had the choice of not joining school activities.

Rush County Schools in Indiana adopted just such a policy. The policy also applied to any student driving to or from school. As in the *Vernonia* case, testing was both suspicionless and random.

Four teenagers and their parents challenged the policy in federal court, and the district court granted summary judgment for the school district. (In a summary judgment decision, a court rules without holding a trial. The court decides that, based on the undisputed facts, one side must win as a matter of law.) The Seventh Circuit Court of Appeals affirmed that decision in early 1998.[6] The Supreme Court chose not to review the case.

In *Willis* v. *Anderson Community School Corporation*[7] and *Joy* v. *Penn-Harris-Madison*

School Corporation,[8] the Seventh Circuit again upheld student drug testing programs. However, the court found that the school in *Joy* had not shown a special need to test student drivers for nicotine. Judge Kenneth Ripple's opinion also noted a desire for more guidance from the Supreme Court.

Meanwhile, other courts heard challenges to student drug testing too. In *Tannahill* v. *Lockney Independent School District*, a federal court in Texas held it was unconstitutional for a school to require drug testing for all students in grades six through twelve. Failure to consent would have led to the loss of a student's good academic standing, as well as disqualification from school activities.[9]

The *Earls* Case in Oklahoma

Tecumseh High School in Oklahoma began testing under its Student Activities Drug Testing Policy in 1999. Consent to urine testing for drugs became a condition for taking part in any extracurricular activity. In practice, however, the school district applied the policy only to competitive activities.

Thus, the Tecumseh policy included student athletes. It also reached groups like the Academic Team, Future Farmers of America, and Future Homemakers of America. Groups like band, choir, and the pom-pom squad fell within the policy too.

Lindsay Earls was a member of show choir, marching band, Academic Team, and National

Honor Society. But she could not take part in those activities unless she agreed to the new drug testing program. Lindsay sued in federal court, together with her sister and parents, plus another student and his mother.

The students lost at the district court level. On appeal, the Tenth Circuit Court of Appeals held that the program was unconstitutional under the Fourth Amendment. The Tenth Circuit held that, among other things, the school district had not shown that it had any substantial drug problem. Nor had the school board shown that drug testing would actually solve any drug problem.[10]

Once again, a split existed between the federal circuit courts on a constitutional issue. The Board of Education appealed to the Supreme Court. In 2002, the Supreme Court heard arguments in *Board of Education of Independent School District No. 92 of Pottawatomie County* v. *Earls*.[11]

During oral argument, Justice Souter took issue with the school's view that a general drug program justified testing students in all activities. "Isn't there at least an equally good argument for testing everybody in the school?" he asked. But if that were true, Justice Souter added, "it seems to me that the concept of special need seems to have gotten lost."

Justice O'Connor worried that the program targeted only students participating in activities, who were least likely to use drugs. "And it seems so odd to try to penalize those students and leave untested the students that are most apt to be engaged in the problem," she said. "It's so counterintuitive, isn't it?" ("Counterintuitive" means going against what seems to make sense.)

"The danger is getting young people used to a drug culture," Justice Scalia noted. "You're raising young people in school." Meanwhile, Justice Breyer asked if the criminal law model of individualized suspicion should even apply. "Nobody is arrested," he told the students' lawyer, Graham Boyd. "This is counseling."

Meanwhile, Justice Souter challenged the argument that the students had a choice about testing:

> They agree to it only under the circumstances that if they don't agree to it, they can't engage in any of these activities. They know perfectly well they'll never get into a competitive college if they don't. . . . There's tremendous pressure on them to agree to it.

In contrast, Justice Kennedy seemed to feel that students who were offended by drug testing did not care about making sure their schools were drug-free. "And there are rights of other children who want to go to a school which is drug-free, if they can," Justice Kennedy stressed.

Indeed, he said, suppose a school district set up two schools. One would require drug testing for all students. The other would have no drug testing, sniffing dogs, or anything else to stop drug use.

"Would that be constitutional?" he challenged the students' lawyer. "And then your client could go to the druggie school."[12]

Board of Education v. Earls— The Majority View

Board of Education v. *Earls* upheld the school district's policy. However, the Court's justices split five to four. Justice Clarence Thomas wrote the majority opinion. Justices Rehnquist, Scalia, Kennedy, and Breyer joined in.

"Because this Policy reasonably serves the School District's important interest in detecting and preventing drug use among its students, we hold that it is constitutional," wrote Justice Thomas.

> A student's privacy interest is limited in a public school environment where the State is responsible for maintaining discipline, health, and safety. . . . Securing order in the school environment sometimes requires that students be subjected to greater controls than those appropriate for adults.[13]

In contrast to the student athletes in *Vernonia*, children in nonathletic activities did not have regular physicals or communal locker rooms. In other words, they had higher privacy expectations. However, that point was "not essential" for the majority in *Earls*. Rather, the issue was "the school's custodial responsibility and authority."[14]

In the majority's view, the sample collection process was "minimally intrusive." Boys could

These are the Supreme Court justices who heard Lindsay Earls's case in 2002. They upheld the school district's drug testing policy.

even urinate inside a closed stall if they preferred. The policy also called for the school to keep test results confidential and separate from other student records. Plus, the school did not turn test results over to any law enforcement agency.

In practice, the students had argued, the school was careless in protecting the information. They gave the example of a choir teacher reading student prescription lists. Despite that, the majority concluded that any invasion of student privacy was "not significant."[15]

Unlike the *Vernonia* case, the record did not show any epidemic drug problem in the Tecumseh schools. Yet the majority found "sufficient evidence" of some drug use. In any case, school districts did not need to wait until drug use was widespread before taking steps to stop it.

"Given the nationwide epidemic of drug use, and the evidence of increased drug use in Tecumseh schools," Justice Thomas wrote, "it was entirely reasonable for the School District to enact this particular drug testing policy."[16] The Tecumseh testing program was "reasonably effective" for preventing and detecting drug use.

This went beyond the *Vernonia* case, which had stressed tailoring that drug testing program to student athletes. The *Earls* majority did not require a direct link between an identifiable drug abuse problem and the group being tested—students in school activities.

The Court in *Earls* also rejected the need for any individualized suspicion of wrongdoing. Besides putting an additional burden on school personnel, a testing program based on suspicion ran the risk that schools might target members of unpopular groups. Additionally, the fear of lawsuits claiming unfair treatment could chill enforcement and make any plan ineffective.

Apparently, the majority did not want to decide just how much drug use would be enough to justify student drug testing under the Constitution. Rather, the justices seemed willing to defer to the local school board's legislative determination.

Although the Court did not say so, some justices may have been concerned about having federal courts get into the business of making policy decisions for local school boards. Generally, courts are supposed to interpret laws, not make them. Plus, while the federal government plays a large role, matters of education have traditionally been the domain of state and local governments. This is based on the Tenth Amendment, which reserves to the states and people the powers not otherwise delegated to the federal government.

Under *Earls,* a school's drug testing plan did not have to be the least intrusive one possible. It just had to be reasonable.

Justice Breyer's Concurring Opinion

Justice Stephen Breyer wrote a short concurring opinion in the *Earls* case. He noted that some people might disagree about whether the testing program was a negligible intrusion on students' privacy. However, the school board had addressed different views by holding public hearings. Plus, the program also did not subject the entire school to testing. Anyone who had serious objections could still refuse testing for a price—giving up school activities.[17]

Justice Breyer also felt that schools did not need grounds to suspect drug use before testing a student. He agreed with the majority that a suspicion requirement could cause schools to single out students in unpopular groups. Testing then could stigmatize students. In other words, it could cloud them with shame or disgrace. Faced with that alternative, Breyer preferred random, suspicionless drug testing.

Board of Education v. Earls— Dissenting Views

Justice Sandra Day O'Connor wrote a one-paragraph dissenting opinion, joined by Justice Souter. They continued to feel that the Court had wrongly decided the *Vernonia* case. In any event, they felt the Tecumseh testing program was unconstitutional even under *Vernonia*.[18]

The dissent written by Justice Ruth Bader Ginsburg elaborated upon this point. Justices O'Connor, Souter, and Stevens joined in that opinion. While the Fourth Amendment allows searches without suspicion if special needs exist, Justice Ginsburg wrote, not every student drug testing program could meet that standard:

> Although "'special needs' inhere in the public school context," those needs are not so expansive or malleable [bendable] as to render reasonable

any program of student drug testing a school district elects to install.

In the dissenters' view, the Tecumseh testing program was not just unreasonable. It was "capricious, even perverse." Unlike the Vernonia schools, the Tecumseh schools did not have a major drug problem. Plus, by testing students in school activities, the policy targeted the students who were least likely to use drugs.[19]

While the majority opinion cited risks of drug use, the dissent felt those risks existed for all schoolchildren. And while school activities have some voluntary aspects, they are still a central part of school life. Students take part in order to enjoy the full advantages of education. Plus, school activities in general did not present the same risks of injury that student athletes faced. The Vernonia schools tailored their program to deal with a perceived danger. The Tecumseh schools did not.

To counter this argument, the school district had listed some situations that could lead to accidents. Band members perform complicated marching routines with heavy musical instruments. Future Farmers of America members might handle animals weighing up to fifteen hundred pounds. The federal government, as *amicus curiae,* also noted that Future Homemakers of America members often handled cutlery or other sharp instruments. However, Ginsburg wrote, none of this justified the drug testing program's broad sweep:

> Notwithstanding nightmarish images of out-of-control flatware, livestock run amok, and colliding tubas disturbing the peace and quiet of Tecumseh, the great majority of students the School District seeks to test in truth are engaged in activities that are not safety sensitive to an unusual degree. There is a difference between imperfect tailoring and no tailoring at all.[20]

Nor, in the dissent's view, was the program saved by the school district's desire to take a strong stand against drug abuse.

Another problem dealt with a procedural issue. The students complained about the way that confidential information was handled by the school. The school board said there was no problem. Instead of holding a trial, the district court ruled in favor of the school district as a matter of law.

The majority in the *Earls* case felt that was all right. However, the dissenters felt, federal court rules at least called for a trial on the disputed fact questions. Otherwise, they believed, it was as if the way the school district carried out its policy made no difference.

In short, the *Earls* case upheld the school district's broad testing policy. But it went far beyond the *Vernonia* case. The Court's five-to-four split suggests the debate is not over yet.

chapter 8

Issues Today

The Supreme Court's ruling in *Earls* seems to leave the door wide open for student drug testing programs. Yet the Court's split suggests the question is not entirely settled. Meanwhile, supporters and opponents of student drug testing continue to debate the wisdom of such policies. Indeed, most schools in the United States still do not have drug testing programs.[1]

Ongoing Issues for the Courts

The *Earls* case noted that students could still opt out of drug testing by giving up school activities. And at least one lower federal court has rejected a policy that would have made drug testing mandatory for all students in grades six and up.[2]

Short of that, it is unclear just how far a school district could go. To what extent can a school district pick and choose among which activities' participants must undergo drug testing? Could schools make drug testing a condition for signing up for any elective (not required) classes? At what point would a student be giving up not just an optional benefit but a critical part of a high-quality public education? These are all open questions.

The actual application of student drug testing policies may lead to other challenges. The majority in the *Earls* case presumed there was no problem with how the school treated confidential information. If schools disregard their own written policies, however, students might argue that they have been denied due process under the Fifth and Fourteenth Amendments. Various cases have said that the government cannot use evidence found when the government failed to follow its own rules. That could make some schools' drug testing unconstitutional under the Fourth Amendment as well.

The scope of drug testing might also become an issue. Some schools have programs that include scanning for nicotine. However, a high school student who is already eighteen can buy tobacco lawfully. And in most places, it is not a crime for someone younger to smoke cigarettes outside of school. While smoking is certainly unhealthy, these factors may provide grounds for a legal challenge if a school used positive test results for nicotine to keep students out of non-sports clubs. (For sports, schools could argue that smoking hinders athletic performance.)

State court rulings could take different directions too. Most state court constitutions have their own versions of the Fourth Amendment. And each state's highest court has the final say over how to interpret and apply those provisions.

States often follow the lead of federal courts in interpreting state constitutional limits on unreasonable searches and seizures. Thus, a New Jersey Supreme Court case upheld Hunterdon Central Regional High School's drug testing program. The program covered students in all extracurricular activities and sports, plus students with parking permits. The court noted that New Jersey's law regarding searches at public schools "generally has mirrored federal law."[3]

Likewise, an Oregon appeals court held that a drug testing program for student athletes did not violate the state constitution.[4] A Texas appeals court upheld a drug testing program for all students in extracurricular activities.[5] And even before *Earls,* the Indiana Supreme Court said it did not go against the state's Search and Seizure Clause for a school to require drug testing for anyone in voluntary activities, even if they got class credit for participation.[6]

In contrast, a Pennsylvania Supreme Court case held that drug testing for all students in extracurricular activities went against the state constitution. The school board in that case had failed to show that there was an actual drug problem or any special need for testing that group of students. Thus, the drug testing was "unreasonable given the heightened protection of privacy under the Pennsylvania Constitution."[7]

Similarly, the Colorado Supreme Court held in a 1998 case that a drug testing program for all students in extracurricular activities from grades six through twelve went against the Fourth Amendment.[8] The U.S. Supreme Court's ruling in the *Earls* case took the opposite view. However, another case might still reject random drug testing under Colorado's state constitution.

Ongoing Policy Debates

Beyond court challenges, the debate on student drug testing will likely shift to the policy arena. Federal courts have held that various student drug testing programs pass constitutional muster. That does not necessarily mean that the programs are a wise use of public resources.

On the one hand, the Department of Education makes grants available to some school districts, and other sources may provide funds as well. Meanwhile, groups like the Student Drug-Testing

Coalition continue to praise the benefits of student drug testing. Analytical labs promote testing in schools too, which helps them get business.

At the same time, opponents like the American Civil Liberties Union and the Drug Policy Alliance argue against the wisdom of student drug testing. They try to persuade students, parents, and school board members with materials such as their pamphlet, *Making Sense of Student Drug Testing: Why Educators Are Saying No.*[9]

One survey soon after the *Earls* case showed wide variations in opinion among educators. Schools also varied greatly in their practices concerning student drug testing and other security measures.[10] Those differences and the policy debate will likely continue.

Meanwhile, research about the effectiveness of student drug testing is ongoing. As experts learn more about the effects of student drug testing programs, policy makers will have a firmer factual foundation for their decisions.

The Future of Student Rights

The Supreme Court's decisions also raise more general questions about the future of student rights. The "special needs" analysis that began with *New Jersey* v. *T.L.O.* is still evolving. In both the *Vernonia* and the *Earls* cases, a majority of the Supreme Court was willing to defer to public

While courts have upheld programs that test athletes and others in extracurricular activities, at least one federal court has rejected a district's policy that would test all middle and high school students.

schools' perceived need to maintain discipline and deter drug use among students.

Many schools have strict zero-tolerance policies to control drugs and violence. In other words, schools make it clear that students cannot possess certain items or engage in threatening conduct at school. Any violations, even minor ones, lead to automatic disciplinary action. Thus, a student who uses a pocketknife to help a teacher pry out a stuck computer disk can get the same punishment as someone who tries to stab another student. Or the victim in a fight might find himself suspended along with the bully who started it.[11]

The *Earls* case's deference to the local school board's judgment could make courts more reluctant to limit such policies. On the other hand, the *Earls* case stressed the nonpunitive nature of the drug testing program. Severe penalties, such as suspension or expulsion, definitely punish students. In 1975, the Supreme Court held that schools cannot deny students their basic right to an education without due process.[12] Thus, courts could still act to prevent unreasonable results.

Other issues arise when schools invite law enforcement officers in to help maintain order.[13] It is unclear how far the *Earls* case might support a relaxed standard for suspicion and reasonableness when police conduct a search and seizure on school property. The *Earls* case showed strong support for schools' efforts to provide a safe and drug-free place for learning. However, the argument that the school acts in place of the parent seems harder to make when police are present. Plus, police searches seem more likely to lead to criminal charges.

As a separate matter, the Supreme Court's makeup changes as presidents appoint new justices. New appointees may hold different views. Thus, future cases might take a different direction.

For now, people on both sides will continue to debate the issue of student drug testing. Likewise, the scope of Fourth Amendment privacy rights and students' constitutional rights in general remain hot topics for debate.

As new controversies arise, courts have to decide those issues. Meanwhile, the more you know about your rights at school and elsewhere, the better you will be able to stand up for those rights for yourself and others.

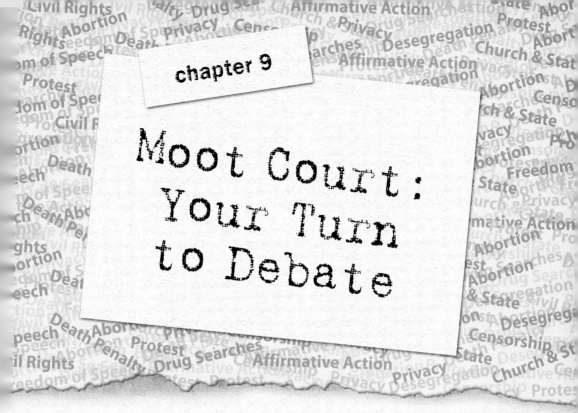

chapter 9

Moot Court: Your Turn to Debate

Law students use practice activities to develop courtroom skills. Mock trials are pretend trials. "Lawyers" present evidence, "witnesses" testify on the stand, "judges" make rulings, and "jurors" decide a case.

Moot court is pretend appellate court work. Students get the facts of a hypothetical case and the trial court's ruling. They do research, write briefs, and argue legal issues before a make-believe panel of appeals court judges. The exercise hones research, writing, and debate skills.

Try a moot court activity with your class or club.[1] This activity deals with drug testing in schools. You can use the format to debate other legal issues too.

Step 1: Assign Roles

If your group has fewer than ten people, everyone can work on one set of briefs and arguments. If you have more than ten people, have several sets of teams. Here are the roles you need to fill:

◇ Judges. If the group is large enough, have nine justices like the Supreme Court. Otherwise, have a panel of three appellate court judges. Choose one person to be Chief Justice and direct the proceedings. The judges hear the attorneys' arguments, question them, and then write and deliver the final ruling. The court's majority opinion is the position agreed upon by a majority of the panel. Individual judges may choose to issue concurring or dissenting opinions. Or, if you can, invite three local lawyers to act as the judges.

◇ Two or more court clerks. They work with the judges to prepare five or more questions to ask the attorneys during oral argument. Clerks also help with research for judges' opinions.

◇ A team of two or more attorneys for the appellant. They feel the lower court was wrong.

◇ A team of two or more attorneys for the appellee. They believe the lower court ruled correctly.

◇ Designated spokespersons for each side. These attorneys present the most persuasive arguments for their side during oral argument. They must also answer questions from the judges.

◇ Two or more reporters. They interview the attorneys before the case and write news stories about the facts of the case and the final ruling.

◇ The bailiff calls the court to order. He or she will also time each side's oral argument.

Step 2: Prepare Your Case: *Norma Teenager* v. *Concerned School Board*

Part 1: Review the Facts and Do Research

A suburban town named Concerned is located in the state of Grace. Statistics on teen drug use worry the local school board. School officials report that students who do not take part in extracurricular activities are more likely to use drugs and get into other types of trouble.

Recently, the Concerned School Board adopted a drug testing program. Testing in the *Earls* case applied to students in extracurricular activities. In contrast, the Concerned program requires urine testing of all high school students who are *not* active in at least one activity. "Active" means that a student must go to 80 percent of group meetings and events, unless excused by a doctor's or parent's note. Students can choose which activity to take part in. However, competitive teams do not have to take everyone who tries out.

Any student covered by the program must submit a urine sample for drug testing by the start of October. After that, Concerned High School will do random drug testing on one fourth of the covered students each month. Procedures for taking samples and doing lab analysis are the same as in the *Earls* case. Steps for reporting and following up on positive test results are the same too.

If a student really objects to drug testing, he or she can choose to get involved in school activities. Thus, the school board feels the program has an element of consent.

Norma Teenager and her parents sued the school board. Norma is a high school sophomore with a 2.5 grade point average. She does not take part in extracurricular activities. She does not want to take part in suspicionless drug testing either. The trial court ruled against Norma. The case is now on appeal.

As background, everyone in the moot court activity should look at the *Earls* case. Your public library may have Supreme Court cases. Look for 536 U.S. 822. That is volume 536 of United States Reports, starting at page 822. If the library carries the Supreme Court Reporter, the *Earls* case is at 122 S.Ct. 2559. You can find the case online too.[2] You may want to do other research also.

These Maine students are participating in a moot court. Such judicial exercises can teach students research, writing, and debating skills.

Part 2: Write Your Briefs

A legal brief is a written presentation of your argument. Brainstorm with the lawyers on your team. How does this case compare to other cases on drug testing? Which arguments are strongest for you? What are your case's weaknesses?

You may want to divide up arguments for research and writing. If so, be sure to work as a team to put the brief together. Otherwise, your brief may have holes or read poorly.

In real life, court rules spell out what briefs must have. Use these rules for your moot court brief:

1. The cover page should have the case name, *Norma Teenager* v. *Concerned School Board.* Say whether it is for appellant or appellee. List the lawyers' names. (This page will not count for the page or word limit.)

2. The text of the brief should have these sections:

   A. Statement of the issue for review: What question is before the court?

   B. Statement of the case: What is this case about? How did the trial court rule?

   C. Statement of the facts: Briefly describe the facts relevant to the case.

   D. Summary of the argument: Sum up your argument in 150 words or less.

   E. Argument: Spell out the legal arguments that support your side. You can divide this into different sections.

Include references to authorities or cases that help your side.

F. Conclusion: Ask the court to rule for your client.

3. Real appeals briefs may be thirty pages long. Limit your brief to no more than five typed pages, double-spaced, or about 1,250 words. If possible, type on a computer. Otherwise, write *very* neatly.

4. On an agreed date, each team gives the other side a copy of its brief. Each judge gets a copy too. If you do this in class, give the teacher a copy. Be sure each team member keeps a copy of the brief also.

In real life, lawyers often prepare reply briefs. You will not do that. But you should be ready to answer the other side's points in oral argument.

Part 3: Prepare for Oral Argument
Each side will have up to fifteen minutes to argue its case. Lawyers should practice their arguments with their teams.

Judges should read all the briefs before oral argument. They should prepare questions for the lawyers.

Step 3: Hold the Oral Argument

Part 1: Assemble the Participants
If your group is small, everyone can watch the oral argument. If you have multiple teams for lawyers for each side, have the judges hear oral arguments

in a separate room with just one set of lawyers for each side present. That way, no one gets an unfair advantage.

◇ The judges sit together in the front of the room. This is the bench. They should not enter until the bailiff calls the court to order. A speaking podium faces the bench.

◇ The appellant's team of attorneys sits on one side, facing the judges.

◇ The appellee's team sits on the opposite side, also facing the judges.

◇ The reporters sit at the back.

◇ As the judges enter, the bailiff calls the court to order: "Oyez (oy-yay)! Oyez! Oyez! The ____ Court of the United States is now in session with the Honorable Chief Judge (or Justice) ___ presiding. All will stand and remain standing until the judges are seated and the Chief Justice has asked all present to be seated." ("Oyez" means "hear ye.")

Part 2: Present the Case

◇ The Chief Justice calls the case and asks whether the parties are ready. Each team's spokesperson answers, "Yes."

◇ The appellant's spokesperson approaches the podium, saying, "May it please the court." Then argument begins. Judges interrupt when they want to asks questions. The attorneys respectfully answer any questions as asked.

Lawyers should not get flustered when a judge interrupts with a question. Instead, they should answer the question honestly, and then move on.

◇ Then the appellee's team takes its turn.

Each team has up to fifteen minutes to present its case. If the appellant's team wants, it can save five minutes of its time to rebut the appellee's argument. If so, the spokesperson should tell the court before sitting down.

◇ After the arguments, the bailiff tells everyone to rise as the judges leave.

◇ At this time, reporters may interview lawyers for the parties and begin working on their articles.

Step 4: Publish and Report on the Decision

After oral argument, the panel of judges decides who wins the case. A majority of the judges must agree on the outcome. If students act as the judges, they should write an opinion explaining their decision. If a judge disagrees, that person can write a dissent.

Limit the length of any opinion to less than five double-spaced typed pages. (Real judges' opinions are often much longer.) Copies of these should go to lawyers for both sides, plus the teacher.

If guest lawyers acted as judges, they do not have to write opinions. However, ask them to tell your group what points persuaded them. They can also award certificates to teams for the best brief and for the best oral argument.

Reporters may interview the lawyers again, if they want. Reporters' stories discussing the case and the outcome are due within twenty-four hours. Limit articles to five hundred words or less.

1. Should upward or downward trends in teen substance abuse affect the reasonableness of student drug testing programs? Suppose, for example, that use of marijuana goes down nationwide, even in states that have very few student drug testing programs. Alternatively, suppose that use of alcohol or other hard-to-detect substances goes up. Would either development affect your views on drug testing? Or should courts simply defer to school boards on the issue?

2. Under the *Vernonia* case, schools can tailor a drug testing program to target student athletes. What if a suspicionless drug testing program targeted only one of the following groups at a high school?

    ◇ Students who dress primarily in black more than four days a week or who are otherwise part of a "Goth" group.

    ◇ Students who got a B or better in chemistry.

    ◇ Students who do not normally have an adult at home within an hour of when they usually finish classes or extracurricular activities at school.

◇ Students who have a parent with a criminal record.

In each case, think about what arguments a school board might make to support drug testing. Then decide what considerations argue against drug testing in each case.

3. Suppose that the Pure Written School Board has a pregnancy testing program for all girls over age eleven. Unless girls and their parents consent to testing every three months, female students cannot take part in sports or other school activities. The school board reasons as follows:

◇ Medical complications occur more often with teen pregnancies. Testing will identify girls who need prenatal care.

◇ In a few notorious cases, desperate girls hid their pregnancies. Then they killed or abandoned their babies. Pregnancy testing might help avoid such tragedies.

◇ Testing will remind students about the problems of teen pregnancies. Many women who have children as teenagers face financial and other social problems. And if a girl has an abortion, some experts worry that psychological problems might follow from feelings of guilt, regret, or hurt.

⬧ Testing might reduce teen pregnancies and sexually transmitted diseases. Testing would be another reason to say "no" to premarital sex. At a minimum, girls would have another basis to insist on condoms for safer sex.

Sixteen-year-old Polly Hanna has sued to stop the Pure Written program. How might court rulings in drug testing cases support the policy? How would you argue against it?

Chapter Notes

Chapter 1. Putting Students to the Test

1. Mark Walsh, "Testing the Limits of School Drug Tests," *Education Week*, March 13, 2002, pp. 1, 13.

2. "High School Students Daniel James and Lindsay Earls and ACLU Attorney Graham Boyd Talk about the Drug-testing Policy of Tecumseh High School in Oklahoma City," CBS News Transcripts, *CBS This Morning*, August 20, 1999.

3. "High School Student in Tecumseh, Oklahoma, Files a Lawsuit in Federal Court over Mandatory Drug Testing of students in Extracurricular Activities," *National Public Radio, Morning Edition*, August 18, 1999. See also "One Test Goody-goody Students Can't Study For," *Pittsburgh Post-Gazette*, July 9, 2002, p. C2; David G. Savage, "Student Drug Test Law Valid," *Los Angeles Times*, June 28, 2002, Sec. 1, p. 1.

4. Jacques Steinberg, "Expanded School Drug Tests Face a Challenge," *New York Times*, August 18, 1999, p. A17.

5. Kathleen Burge, "Salem Schools Chief Proposes Random Drug Tests for Some Students," *Boston Globe*, January 13, 2005, p. B5.

6. Jules Crittenden, "Haverhill Considers School Drug Testing," *Boston Herald*, January 29, 2005, p. 13.

7. "Parents, Not Schools, Should Drug-Test Children," *Tampa Tribune*, April 3, 2004, p. 16.

8. Erik Nielsen, "School to Start Drug Testing," *Idaho Falls Post Register*, September 28, 2005, p. A1.

9. Marissa Alanis, "Heritage Begins Drug Testing," *Dallas Morning News*, September 15, 2005, p. 5B.

10. Sheena Dooley, "Homestead Starts Random Drug Testing," *News-Sentinel*, September 15, 2005, p. 1L.

11. "New Jersey Adopts Student Testing Provisions," *Workplace Substance Abuse Advisor*, September 15, 2005.

12. Laurel Walker, "Drug Tests in Schools May Not Be So Useful," *Milwaukee Journal Sentinel*, April 22, 2004, p. 1B.

13. SB 1386, Senate Bill—Veto, September 18, 2004, <http://info.sen.ca.gov/pub/03-04/bill/sen/sb_1351-1400/sb_1386_vt_20040918.html> (February 28, 2005). See also Jim Sanders, "Drug Tests in Schools a Hot Issue," *Sacramento Bee*, July 5, 2004, p. A3.

14. Peter Schworm, "High School Adopts Alcohol Test," *Boston Globe*, October 3, 2004, p. 16.

15. Judy Laurinatis, "Drug Testing: Touted as Deterrent," *Pittsburgh Post-Gazette*, August 18, 2004, p. EZ-4; Judy Laurinatis, "Drug Testing to Start in Fall," *Pittsburgh Post-Gazette*, August 4, 2004, p. EZ-4.

16. *Vernonia School District 47J* v. *Acton*, 515 U.S. 646 (1995).

17. *Board of Education* v. *Earls*, 536 U.S. 822 (2002).

Chapter 2. Drugs in Schools—A Nationwide Problem

1. D. Wright and N. Sathe, *State Estimates of Substance Use from the 2002–2003 National Surveys on Drug Use and Health* (Rockville, MD: Substance Abuse and Mental Health Services Administration, January 2005), pp. 2–3, 31.

2. University of Michigan, "Overall Teen Drug Use Continues Gradual Decline; But Use of Inhalants Rises," December 21, 2004, pp. 13, 19, <http://www.nida.nih.gov/Newsroom/04/2004MTFDrug.pdf> (April 4, 2005).

3. D. Wright and N. Sathe, pp. 4, 52, 64, 66.

4. National Highway Traffic Safety Administration, National Center for Statistics and Analysis, "Alcohol Involvement in Fatal Motor Vehicle Traffic Crashes, 2003," March 2005, p. 1, <http://www-nrd.nhtsa.dot.gov/pdf/nrd-30/NCSA/Rpts/2005/809822.pdf> (April 4, 2005);

National Highway Traffic Safety Administration, National Center for Statistics and Analysis, "State Alcohol Related Fatality Rates 2003," February 2005, p. 1, <http://www-nrd .nhtsa.dot.gov/pdf/nrd-30/NCSA/Rpts/2005/809830.pdf> (April 4, 2005).

5. National Highway Traffic Safety Administration, "Traffic Safety Facts: 2003 Data," 2004, p. 2, <http://www-nrd. nhtsa.dot.gov/pdf/nrd-30/NCSA/TSF2003/809761.pdf> (April 4, 2005).

6. Bureau of Justice Statistics, "Drugs and Crime Facts: Drug Use and Crime," January 13, 2005, <http://www. ojp.usdoj.gov/bjs/dcf/duc.htm> (April 4, 2005).

7. MADD, "Stats and Resources: Did You Know?" n.d., <http://www.madd.org/stats/0,1056,1789,00.html> (April 4, 2005).

8. Robert L. DuPont, Teresa G. Campbell, and Jacqueline J. Mazza, "Report of a Preliminary Study: Elements of a Successful School-Based Student Drug Testing Program," Institute for Behavior and Health, Inc., July 22, 2002, p. 2, <http://www.datia.org/pdf_resources/ prelim_study.pdf> (April 4, 2005); "A Timeline of Drug Testing in the United States," September 19, 2002, <http://www.hightimes.com/ht/legal/content.php?bid=131 &aid=3> (April 19, 2005).

9. Kenneth D. Tunnell, *Pissing on Demand: Workplace Drug Testing and the Rise of the Detox Industry* (New York: New York University Press, 2004), p. 23.

10. DuPont, Campbell, and Mazza.

11. Brown University Health Education, "Alcohol and Your Body," February 7, 2005, <http://www.brown.edu/ Student_Services/Health_Services/Health_Education/atod/ alc_aayb.htm> (April 4, 2005).

12. David J. Hanson, "Breathalyzer Accuracy and DWI/DUI Conviction Rates," 1997–2004, <http://www2.

potsdam.edu/alcohol-info/DrivingIssues/1093825780.html>
(April 5, 2004).

13. Tom Mieczkowski, ed., *Drug Testing Technology: Assessment of Field Applications* (Boca Raton, Fla.: CRC Press, 1999), p. 111; American BioMedica Corp., "About Drug Testing," n.d., <http://www.drugfreeschools.com/drugtesting.html> (March 31, 2005).

14. *Vernonia School District 47J v. Acton,* 515 U.S. 646, 651 (1995).

15. Mieczkowski, pp. 283–346.

16. George S. Yacoubian, "To Pee or Not to Pee: School Drug Testing in an Era of Oral Fluid Analysis," 2003, <http://www.criminology.fsu.edu/journal/schooldrug.htm> (September 30, 2005).

17. Office of National Drug Control Policy, *What You Need to Know About Starting a Student Drug-Testing Program* (Washington, D.C.: Office of National Drug Control Policy, 2004), p. 16.

18. Joseph R. McKinney, "Effectiveness of Random Student Drug-Testing Programs: 2005," August 2005, <http://www.studentdrugtesting.org/2005%20McKinney%20survey%20results.pdf> (September 28, 2005); Mike Jackson, "Another Texas High School District to Begin Steroid Testing," *Dallas Morning News,* March 25, 2005, p. 1B. See also Accu-Chem Laboratories, "Student Drug Testing," n.d., <http://www.accuchem.com/doa/schoolfaq.htm> (September 29, 2005).

Chapter 3. Arguments for Student Drug Testing

1. George W. Bush, State of the Union Address, January 20, 2004, <http://www.whitehouse.gov/news/releases/2004/01/20040120-7.html> (February 13, 2005). See also "President's State of the Union Address to Congress and the Nation," *New York Times,* January 21, 2004, p. 18.

2. Office of National Drug Control Policy, "Executive Summary," *National Drug Control Strategy, FY 2006:*

Budget Summary, February 2005, p. 2, <http://www. whitehousedrugpolicy.gov/publications/policy/06budget/ exec_summ.pdf> (April 4, 2005).

3. National Institute on Drug Abuse, "Teen Drug Use Declines 2003–2004—But Concerns Remain About Inhalants and Painkillers," press release, December 21, 2004, <http://www.drugabuse.gov/newsroom/04/NR12-21. html> (February 15, 2005).

4. "Ask the White House," January 7, 2005, <http:// www.whitehouse.gov/ask/20050107.html> (January 7, 2005).

5. Linn Goldberg, et al., "Drug Testing Athletes to Prevent Substance Abuse: Background and Pilot Study Results of the SATURN (Student Athletes Testing Using Random Notification) Study," *Journal of Adolescent Health,* January 2003, pp. 16–25.

6. Linn Goldberg, e-mail communication to author, February 13, 2005.

7. Linn Goldberg, et al.

8. Joseph R. McKinney, "The Effectiveness and Legality of Random Drug Testing Policies," n.d., <http://www.datia. org/pdf_resources/IN%20survey.PDF> (February 20, 2005); Joseph R. McKinney, "The Effectiveness of Random Drug Testing Programs: A Statewide Follow-up Study," n.d., <http://www.studentdrugtesting.org/McKinney%20follow% 20up%20study.PDF> (February 20, 2005).

9. Joseph R. McKinney, "Effectiveness of Random Student Drug-Testing Programs: 2005," August 2005, <http://www.studentdrugtesting.org/2005%20McKinney%2 0survey%20results.pdf> (September 28, 2005).

10. Robert L. DuPont, Teresa G. Campbell, and Jacqueline J. Mazza, "Report of a Preliminary Study: Elements of a Successful School-Based Student Drug Testing Program," Institute for Behavior and Health, Inc.,

July 22, 2002, pp. 14–15, <http://www.datia.org/pdf_resources/prelim_study.pdf> (April 4, 2005).

11. Cheryl N. Schmidt, "Polk Schools Laud Testing of Athletes for Drug Use," *Tampa Tribune*, June 2, 2004, p. 1.

12. Office of National Drug Control Policy, *National Drug Control Strategy* (Washington, D.C.: U.S. Government Printing Office, March 2004), pp. 14–15; Office of National Drug Control Policy, *What You Need to Know About Drug Testing in Schools* (Washington, D.C.: U.S. Government Printing Office, 2002), p. 12.

13. Ryoko Yamaguchi, Lloyd D. Johnston, and Patrick M. O'Malley, "Relationship Between Student Illicit Drug Use and School Drug-Testing Policies," *Journal of School Health*, April 2003, p. 159.

14. Office of National Drug Control Policy, *National Drug Control Strategy;* and Office of National Drug Control Policy, *What You Need to Know About Drug Testing in Schools.*

15. "Ask the White House."

16. Joseph R. McKinney, "Study of High Schools with Student Drug Testing Programs," 2004, <http://www.studentdrugtesting.org/2004%20MCKINNEY%20STUDY.PDF> (February 22, 2005).

17. Kathleen Burge, "Spurred by Son's Addiction, Educator Pushes Drug Testing," *Boston Globe*, January 18, 2005, p. A1.

18. Joseph R. McKinney, "Effectiveness of Random Student Drug-Testing Programs: 2005."

19. *Northwestern Sch. Corp. v. Linke*, 763 N.E.2d 972, 984 (2002); Ralph D. Mawdsley, "Random Drug Testing for Extracurricular Activities: Has the Supreme Court Opened Pandora's Box for Public Schools?" *Brigham Young University Education and Law Journal*, 2003, pp. 587, 608.

20. Office of National Drug Control Policy, *What You Need to Know About Starting a Student Drug-testing*

Program (Washington, D.C.: Office of National Drug Control Policy, 2004), p. 19.

21. Amy Greene, "Students' Suit Stirs Tecumseh; National Spotlight Hard to Avoid," *Daily Oklahoman,* August 25, 1999.

Chapter 4. Arguments Against Student Drug Testing

1. *Tinker* v. *Des Moines Independent Community School Dist.,* 393 U.S. 503, 506 (1969), cited in *Vernonia School District 47J v. Acton,* 515 U.S. 646, 655–56 (1995), and *Board of Education* v. *Earls,* 536 U.S. 822, 829 (2002).

2. *Vernonia School District No. 47J v. Acton,* 515 U.S. 646, 680 (1995) (O'Connor, J., dissenting).

3. Drug Policy Alliance, "U.S. Supreme Court Strips Privacy Rights from Millions of U.S. Students," press release, June 27, 2002, <http://www.commondreams.org/news2002/0627-08.htm> (February 22, 2005).

4. *Trinidad School District No. 1* v. *Lopez,* 963 P.2d 1095, 1100, 1108 (Colo. 1998). See also Jacob L. Brooks, "Suspicionless Drug Testing of Students Participating in Non-athletic Competitive School Activities: Are All Students Next?" *Wyoming Law Review,* 2004, pp. 365, 386.

5. Ryoko Yamaguchi, Lloyd D. Johnston, and Patrick M. O'Malley, "Relationship Between Student Illicit Drug Use and School Drug-Testing Policies," *Journal of School Health,* April 2003, p. 159.

6. Paul Armentano, "Pull the Plug on Student Drug Tests," *Tampa Tribune,* March 30, 2004, p. 9.

7. Laurel Walker, "Drug Tests in Schools May Not Be So Useful," *Milwaukee Journal Sentinel,* April 22, 2004, p. 1B.

8. Fatema Gunja, et al., *Making Sense of Student Drug Testing* (New York: Drug Policy Alliance and American Civil Liberties Union, January 2004), p. 10, <http://www.

drugtestingfails.org/pdf/drug_testing_booklet.pdf> (April 4, 2005).

9. Nicholas A. Palumbo, "Protecting Access to Extracurricular Activities: The Need to Recognize a Fundamental Right to a Minimally Adequate Education," *Brigham Young University Education and Law Journal*, 2004, pp. 393, 394.

10. *Joy* v. *Penn-Harris-Madison School Corp.*, 212 F.3d 1052, 1067 (7th Cir. 2000).

11. Debra J. Saunders, "Want to Join the Chess Club? Pee in a Cup," *San Francisco Chronicle*, July 4, 2002, p. A22.

12. *Theodore* v. *Delaware Valley Sch. Dist.*, 575 Pa. 321, 347-48, 836 A.2d 76, 92 (2003), citing N. Zill, C. Nord, and L. Loomis, *Adolescent Time Use, Risky Behavior and Outcomes: An Analysis of National Data* (Westate, Inc., 1995), p. 52. See also Brooks, pp. 365, 390–401; Palumbo, p. 394; Kimberly Menashe Glassman, "Shedding Their Rights: The Fourth Amendment and Suspicionless Drug Testing of Public School Students Participating in Extracurricular Activities," *Catholic University Law Review*, Spring 2002, pp. 951, 981–983.

13. 536 U.S. 822 (2002).

14. *Board of Education* v. *Earls*, Brief of Amici Curiae American Academy of Pediatrics, National Education Association, et al., 2001 U.S. Briefs 332 (February 6, 2002). See also M. Casey Kucharson, "Please Report to the Principal's Office, Urine Trouble: The Effect of Board of Education v Earls on America's Schoolchildren," *Akron Law Review*, 2004, pp. 131, 165–169.

15. "Ban School Drug Tests," *San Francisco Chronicle*, June 30, 2004, p. B8.

16. *West Virginia Board of Education* v. *Barnette*, 319 U.S. 624, 637 (1943) (Jackson, J.), cited in *Board of Education* v. *Earls*, 536 U.S. 822, 855 (Ginsburg, J.,

dissenting), and *Theodore v. Delaware Valley Sch. Dist.,* 575 Pa. 321, 354, 836 A.2d 76, 95-96 (2003). See also Brooks, pp. 365, 381–382, 387–389.

Chapter 5. The Legal Context of Student Drug Testing

1. Layli Whyte, "Schools to Begin Random Drug Testing," *The Hub* (Red Bank, N.J.), September 9, 2005, <http://hub.gmnews.com/news/2005/0909/Front_Page/003.html> (October 1, 2005); "State Sets Uniform Drug Test Rules," *Home News Tribune Online,* August 31, 2005, <http://www.thnt.com/apps/pbcs.dll/article?AID=/20050831/NEWS/508310394/1001 (October 1, 2005); "Sacco Pleased Codey Signs His Drug Testing Bill for Student Athletes," *News from New Jersey State Democrats,* August 29, 2005, <http://www.njsendems.com/Releases/05/August/Sacco%20Pleased%20Codey%20Signs%20his%20Drug%20Testing%20Bill%20for%20Student%20Athletes,%208-29-05.htm> (October 1, 2005).

2. "Congress Proposes Drug Testing of All High School Students," Summer 1999, <http://www.ndsn.org/summer99/test1.html> (March 31, 2005).

3. No Child Left Behind Act of 2001, Public Law 107–110, Section 4115(b)(2)(E)(xiv), 115 Stat. 1425, 1748–49 (January 8, 2002).

4. Martha Jacobs, U.S. Department of Education, e-mail communication to author, March 28, 2006.

5. U.S. Department of Education, *Fiscal Year 2007 Budget Summary and Background Information,* 2006, pp. 32–33, <http://www.ed.gov/about/overview/budget/budget07/summary/07summary.pdf> (March 30, 2006).

6. Office of National Drug Control Policy, "Department of Education," *National Drug Control Strategy, FY 2006: Budget Summary,* February 2005, p. 3, <http://www.whitehousedrugpolicy.gov/publications/policy/06budget/education.pdf> (April 4, 2005).

7. *Terry* v. *Ohio*, 392 U.S. 1 (1968). See also Brad Setterbeg, "Privacy Changes, Precedent Doesn't: Why *Board of Education* v. *Earls* Was Judged by the Wrong Standard," *Houston Law Review*, Winter 2003, pp. 1183, 1198–1201.

8. *United States* v. *Martinez-Fuerte*, 428 U.S. 543 (1976).

9. *Tinker* v. *Des Moines Independent Community School Dist.*, 393 U.S. 503, 506 (1969).

10. *New Jersey* v. *T.L.O.*, 469 U.S. 325 (1985).

11. 469 U.S. at 340.

12. Ibid. See also M. Casey Kucharson, "Please Report to the Principal's Office, Urine Trouble: The Effect of Board of Education v Earls on America's Schoolchildren," *Akron Law Review*, 2004, pp. 131, 137–138.

13. 469 U.S. at 385.

14. Ralph D. Mawdsley, "Random Drug Testing for Extracurricular Activities: Has the Supreme Court Opened Pandora's Box for Public Schools?" *Brigham Young University Education and Law Journal*, 2003, pp. 587, 602–603; Todd A. DeMitchell and Casey D. Cobb, "Policy Responses to Violence in Our Schools: An Exploration of Security as a Fundamental Value," *Brigham Young University Education and Law Journal*, 2003, pp. 459, 469–470.

Chapter 6. Round One in the Courts

1. *Skinner* v. *Railway Labor Executives' Assn.*, 489 U.S. 602 (1989).

2. 489 U.S. at 636.

3. *Treasury Employees* v. *Von Raab*, 489 U.S. 656, 670 (1989).

4. 489 U.S. at 680-81.

5. 864 F.2d 1309 (7th Cir. 1988).

6. 930 F.2d 915 (5th Cir. 1991).

7. *Vernonia School District 47J* v. *Acton*, 515 U.S. 646, 648–49 (1995).

8. Harry Lenhart, "ACLU of Oregon, Faces of Liberty: James Acton," n.d., <http://www.aclu-or.org/faces/acton. html> (February 3, 2005); "Mandatory Drug Tests of Student Athletes Sought," *The Legal Intelligencer*, March 29, 1995, p. 4.

9. *Vernonia School District 47J* v. *Acton*, oral argument, 1995 U.S. Trans Lexis 84, March 28, 1995, pp. 4, 7–8, 11, 36, 43, 48. See also Joan Buskupic, "Supreme Court Looks into the Locker Room," *Washington Post*, March 29, 1995, p. A9; David G. Savage, "Court Debates School Drug Tests," *Chicago Sun-Times*, March 29, 1995, p. 18.

10. 515 U.S. at 652.

11. 515 U.S. at 654–55.

12. 515 U.S. at 657.

13. Ibid. See also Neal Hutchens, "Suspicionless Drug Testing: The Tuition for Attending Public School?" *Alabama Law Review*, Summer 2002, pp. 1265, 1269–70.

14. 515 U.S. at 661–62 (emphasis in original).

15. 515 U.S. at 663.

16. 515 U.S. at 666.

17. 515 U.S. at 667.

18. 515 U.S. at 671.

19. 515 U.S. at 672, citing *Treasury Employees* v. *Von Raab*, 489 U.S. 656, 680 (1989) (Scalia, J., dissenting).

20. *Cupp* v. *Murphy*, 412 U.S. 291, 295 (1973) (Stewart, J.).

21. 515 U.S. at 678 (emphasis in original).

22. 515 U.S. at 686.

23. *New Jersey* v. *T.L.O.*, 469 U.S. 325 (1985), discussed at 515 U.S. 680–81.

Chapter 7. Round Two: Drug Testing Expands

1. *Chandler* v. *Miller*, 520 U.S. 305 (1997).

2. *Ferguson* v. *City of Charleston*, 532 U.S. 67 (2001). See generally Krislen Nalani Chun, "Still Wondering After

All These Years: *Ferguson* v. *City of Charleston* and the Supreme Court's Lack of Guidance over Drug Testing and the Special Needs Doctrine," *Hawaii Law Review*, Summer 2002, p. 797.

3. *Knox County Educ. Ass'n* v. *Knox County Bd. Of Educ.*, 158 F.3d 361 (6th Cir. 1998); *Aubrey* v. *School Board of Lafayette Parish*, 148 F.3d 559 (5th Cir. 1998). *Stigile* v. *Clinton*, 110 F.3d 801 (D.C. Cir. 1997).

4. *Stigile* v. *Clinton*, 110 F.3d 801 (D.C. Cir. 1997).

5. *Wilcher* v. *City of Wilmington*, 139 F.3d 366 (3d Cir. 1998).

6. *Todd* v. *Rush County Schools*, 133 F.3d 974 (7th Cir. 1998), cert. denied 525 U.S. 824 (1998).

7. *Willis* v. *Anderson Community School Corp.*, 158 F.3d 415 (7th Cir. 1998).

8. *Joy* v. *Penn-Harris-Madison School Corp.*, 212 F.3d 1052 (7th Cir. 2000).

9. *Tannahill* v. *Lockney Indep. Sch. Dist.*, 133 F. Supp. 2d 919 (N.D. Tex., 2001).

10. *Earls* v. *Board of Education*, 242 F.2d 1264 (10th Cir., 2001), reversed 536 U.S. 822 (2002).

11. *Board of Education* v. *Earls*, 536 U.S. 822 (2002).

12. *Board of Education* v. *Earls*, oral argument, 2002 U.S. Trans Lexis 30, March 19, 2002, pp. 12–13, 17–18, 21, 25, 28, 32–33, 43, 53. See also Peter Cassidy, "Pee First, Ask Questions Later," *In These Times*, January 20, 2003, p. 10; Mark Cloud, "Our Privacy Stolen One Cup at a Time," *Baltimore Sun*, April 8, 2002, p. 11A; Oyez Supreme Court Multimedia, *Board of Education* v. *Earls*, 2002, <http://www.oyez.org/audio/cases/1493/argument. mp3> (September 28, 2002).

13. 536 U.S. at 825.

14. 536 U.S. at 830–31.

15. 536 at 834.

16. 536 U.S. at 835. See also Brian Kim, "Marijuana or

Football (or the Future Farmers of America): *Board of Education* v. *Earls*, 122 S.Ct. 2559 (2002)," *Harvard Journal of Law & Public Policy*, Summer 2003, pp. 973, 975–978.

17. 536 U.S. at 838–42. See also Kim, pp. 978–979; Irene Merker Rosenberg, "The Public Schools Have a 'Special Need' for Their Students' Urine," *Hofstra Law Review*, Winter 2002, pp. 303, 318–321.

18. 536 U.S. at 842.

19. 536 U.S. at 843.

20. 536 U.S. at 852. See also M. Casey Kucharson, "Please Report to the Principal's Office, Urine Trouble: The Effect of Board of Education v Earls on America's Schoolchildren," *Akron Law Review*, 2004, pp. 131, 157–158, 162; Courtney Donovan, "*Board of Education* v. *Earls:* Has the Supreme Court Gone Too Far on Student Drug Testing?" *Georgetown Journal of Law & Public Policy*, Winter 2004, pp. 337, 345–347.

Chapter 8. Issues Today

1. Andy Sullivan, "More Drug Tests in Schools Urged by White House," *Boston.com*, March 20, 2006, <http://www.boston.com/news/education/k-12/articles/2006/03/20/more_drug_tests_in_schools_urged_by_white_house> (March 30, 2006). See also Jacob L. Brooks, "Suspicionless Drug Testing of Students Participating in Non-athletic Competitive School Activities: Are All Students Next?" *Wyoming Law Review*, 2004, pp. 365, 393–394.

2. *Tannahill* v. *Lockney Indep. Sch. Dist.*, 133 F. Supp. 2d 919 (N.D. Tex., 2001. See also Ralph D. Mawdsley, "Random Drug Testing for Extracurricular Activities: Has the Supreme Court Opened Pandora's Box for Public Schools?" *Brigham Young University Education and Law Journal*, 2003, pp. 587, 600–603; Brooks, pp. 365, 395;

3. *Joye* v. *Hunterdon Central Regional High School*

Board of Education, 176 N.J. 568, 608, 826 A.2d 624, 648 (2003).

4. *Weber* v. *Oakridge School District 76,* 184 Ore. App. 415, 56 P.3d 504 (Ore. App. 2002).

5. *Marble Falls Ind. Sch. Dist.* v. *Shell,* 2003 Tex. App. LEXIS 2845 (2003).

6. *Linke* v. *Northwestern School Corp.,* 763 N.E. 2d 972 (Ind. 2002).

7. *Theodore* v. *Delaware Valley Sch. Dist.,* 575 Pa. 321, 346-47, 836 A.2d 76, 91 (2003). See also Adam T. Wolf, "*Theodore* v. *Delaware Valley School District:* School Drug Testing and Its Limitations under the Pennsylvania Constitution," *Widener Law Journal,* 2005, p. 505.

8. *Trinidad School District No. 1* v. *Lopez,* 963 P.2d 1095, 1100, 1108 (Colo. 1998).

9. Fatema Gunja, et al., *Making Sense of Student Drug Testing* (New York: Drug Policy Alliance and American Civil Liberties Union, January 2004), <http://www.drugtestingfails.org/pdf/drug_testing_booklet.pdf> (April 4, 2005).

10. Cynthia Kelly Conlon, "Urineschool: A Study of the Impact of the *Earls* Decision on High School Random Drug Testing Policies," *Journal of Law & Education,* July 2003, p. 297.

11. Joseph Lintott, "Teaching and Learning in the Face of School Violence," *Georgetown Journal on Poverty Law & Policy,* Fall 2005, pp. 553, 565–567.

12. *Goss* v. *Lopez,* 419 U.S. 565 (1975).

13. Josh Kagan, "Reappraising *T.L.O.*'s 'Special Needs' Doctrine in an Era of School-Law Enforcement Entanglement," *Journal of Law & Education,* July 2004, pp. 291, 304–309; Michael Pinard, "From the Classroom to the Courtroom: Reassessing Fourth Amendment Standards in Public School Searches Involving Law Enforcement Authorities," *Arizona Law Review,* Winter 2003, pp. 1067, 1075–77, 1104–1106; Michael A. Sprow, "The High Price of Safety: May Public Schools Institute a Policy of Frisking

Students as They Enter the Building?" *Baylor Law Review,* Winter 2002, pp. 133–136, 155–157.

Chapter 9. Moot Court: Your Turn to Debate

1. Adapted from Millie Aulbur, "Constitutional Issues and Teenagers," The Missouri Bar, n.d., <http://www. mobar.org/teach/clesson.htm> (January 6, 2005); Street Law Inc. and the Supreme Court Historical Society, "Moot Court Activity," 2002, <http://www.landmarkcases.org/ mootcourt.html> (January 6, 2004); with suggestions from Ron Fridell.

2. Legal Information Institute, *Board of Education* v. *Earls,* and linked pages, <http://straylight.law.cornell. edu/supct/html/01-332.ZO.html> (September 28, 2005). The *Earls* oral argument can be heard at Oyez Supreme Court Multimedia, 2002, <http://www.oyez.org/audio/cases/ 1493/argument.mp3> (September 28, 2002).

Glossary

Breathalyzer—A device for estimating a person's blood alcohol content based on chemicals in the breath.

coercion—Force, compulsion, or intimidation.

depressants—Drugs that slow down the body's metabolism. Examples include alcohol, GHB, sedatives, and tranquilizers.

hallucinogens—Drugs that interfere with users' perceptions of reality.

opiates—Drugs derived from the poppy plant (or synthetic versions of such drugs), including various painkillers.

oral fluids—Saliva and other liquids present in the mouth.

stimulants—Drugs that speed up the body's metabolism. Examples include cocaine, crack, amphetamines, and methamphetamine. Ecstasy, or MDMA, acts as a stimulant and hallucinogen.

urinalysis—Testing of urine to determine the presence of various chemical substances.

Further Reading

Garrett, Brandon. *The Right to Privacy.* New York: Rosen Publishing Group, 2001.

Jasper, Margaret C. *Teenagers and Substance Abuse.* Dobbs Ferry, N.Y.: Oceana Publications, Inc., 2003.

Kowalski, Kathiann M. *Teen Rights: At Home, At School, Online.* Berkeley Heights, N.J.: Enslow Publishers, 2000.

Ramen, Fred. *The Right to Freedom from Searches.* New York: Rosen Publishing Group, 2001.

Roleff, Tamara L., editor. *Drug Abuse: Opposing Viewpoints.* Farmington Hills, Mich.: Greenhaven Press, 2005.

Internet Addresses

American Civil Liberties Union
<http://www.aclu.org>

Drug Policy Alliance, "Drug Testing Fails Our Youth"
<http://www.drugtestingfails.org>

Office of National Drug Control Policy
<http://www.whitehousedrugpolicy.gov>

Student Drug-Testing Coalition
<http://www.studentdrugtesting.org>

Index